THE WIND BLEW INNOCENT

DONNA ARP WEITZMAN

Printed in the United States of America.

First Printing, 2017

Author photograph by Mimi Butler

Cover art by Jeanette Korab

Cover design by Cachet Petty

Other books by Donna Arp Weitzman

Cinderella Has Cellulite and Other Musings of a Last Wife
Sex & the Siren: Tales of a Later Dater
Born to Build: The Story of How Dallas Became a Shopper's
Paradise

To Brandon and Collin. You fill my heart with pride and joy.
Thank you for being my most treasured legacy.
With unending love,
Mom

TABLE OF CONTENTS

For all things good about me, I thank my parents and my siblings. For all things bad, I accept responsibility.

For your interest in a Texas farm girl's unremarkable life, thank you. Every word is from my memory—sometimes bringing tears, clenched jaws, and sadness and at other times bringing joy for the special days we were all together, laughing and playing.

As the Irish say, "May the wind always be at your back."

INTRODUCTION

Claustrophobia. I didn't know the feeling until I moved to Dallas. The city's concrete skyscrapers stifle most breezes and often divert the wind. Breaths of air are more labored and offered less freely compared to life in West Texas where I grew up.

In my new city as a young single adult, I was fortunate to meet wonderful friends and occasionally a lover. Sometimes after dinner my latest beau would wrap me in his arms to kiss goodnight. I was often bothered by prolonged embracing, our bodies being so close would quickly become an irritant to me and led to my pushing him away with a brisk, "Sorry, but I need to breathe!"

Why was that? I've since developed a theory. Growing up, whenever my constant companion the wind would die down, stillness and oppressive humidity would overtake my lungs until I could feel the wind against my cheek again. As I did then, I suddenly needed space for myself...and maybe away from him. Wind equates space, which equates life to me.

Often misreading my cues, my consort would let me go, looking rejected. And there I would be again, another man misunderstanding my need for breath. I never liked kissing for more than a few seconds. The mistreatment of stopping my air supply and suppressing my lifeblood often scared me into pulling away. If a man tried to do it again, I would be uncooperative. He probably thought I didn't like him, and at that moment, I didn't!

There was no rejection—just the familiar feeling of needing the wind in my face, blowing my hair, giving me life and freedom. Of course, wind is different from air. We all breathe air. But wind is aggressive and must be dealt with. In rural Texas where my roots are, the wind doesn't stop for any substantial period. Sometimes it waits for its companions—rain, dirty sleet, and possibly a winter snow—but most days it beats out its competitors and blows unrestricted.

Even with decades of city living behind me now, most of my recollections of childhood involve the wind in one way or another. My bedroom had two drafty windows facing the south. Wind loves the south. I also had two west-facing windows, receiving the winds before oncoming storms that often seemed to originate in the west. This same Texas wind shaped the twists and turns in my complex and messy maturation from childhood to adulthood.

My story starts with my mother, omnipresent and influential in every aspect of my life. As one of the oldest in a family of nine children, she knew the difficulty of raising a large family. She took every precaution against getting pregnant and used to joke, "All your daddy had to do was hang his pants on the bedpost and I would get pregnant." Mother meant every word of it when she told my siblings that every one of us was a mistake, yet she loved us dearly. Instead of scarring us psychologically, her brutal honesty made us feel closer, knowing we were all in the same boat and that our mother had no favorites.

A Blue Norther, what Texans call a kind of blustery storm that brings a sudden drop in temperature, raged on the eve of my December birth—its strong winds blowing ice onto the dark narrow road to the nearest doctor. But Daddy persisted and somehow got Mother to General Hospital in Henrietta, Texas, on time for my arrival. I've always felt a bit special, as I was the youngest and the only sibling in my family born in a hospital.

Much like the albatross needing the wind to lift its heavy wings, the wind always provided the push I needed to make life's changes. So the fact that it accompanied my mom on the way to the hospital on the night of my birth is no surprise. The wind often forces a shift through brute force, and many people take these sinister acts for granted instead of seeing them as potentially providential.

If you grew up in the swamps of Florida, the forests of New England, or the mountains of Colorado, perhaps the wind was less impactful in your life experiences. But for me, the wind sustained my lungs and shoved me forward regularly. A West Texas farm girl, I realized early in life that water was precious on drought-prone land, but it was the wind that we couldn't imagine life without. I didn't worry too much about the future, as the wind would surely provide. At times its anger would accompany tornadoes and snowstorms, but most often it was welcome—blowing in the rain, turning the windmill, and cooling the hot summer nights.

I miss it when I'm walking down a crowded street in New York or feeling stifled by the concrete surrounding my home in the city. Unlike my childhood room, my bedroom windows are sealed shut, thus allowing no gust to enter. So I often open the den windows when it's far too hot or too cold for the breezes. "Close those windows… it's cold," my husband sometimes admonishes me. For only a brief moment, I think of those southern windows in a little girl's bedroom and how the curtains tickled my toes if I allowed them to pop out from under the covers.

I miss the Christmas when my brother brought all our presents into another room away from the drafts howling under the baseboards. I even miss my mother shouting for my dad to "watch those clouds" as she prepared us to spend another quiet night in the storm cellar. Most of all, I miss having so much air to breathe and nothing between a little girl and the innocence of life.

The Cherokee Indians who once roamed my homeland believed that the wind could summon demons to haunt bad souls. But if you were of pure heart, the welcoming wind would bring rain to sustain you. Although I've been told I have only a smidgen of Native American blood, the wind is inextricably part of my family tree. Like a crazy, unpredictable cousin, it's always welcome but sometimes dreaded.

PART 1

Salvation

DADDY NEEDED TO BE SAVED. MOTHER MADE SURE everyone knew Daddy was going to hell if he didn't dunk his body in the baptismal pool. I wasn't sure why Mother was so concerned, but I hoped Daddy wouldn't die before he did so, as I certainly didn't want him to be in hell.

Maybe this is true love? Not wanting your relatives to die in hell?

Evangelicals and right-wing Christians comprised my circle of friends, my parents, our neighbors and 99 percent of all the people I knew growing up in my small town. Most were Baptists, but a few were Methodist and other Christian faiths. I never knew a single Jew, much less a practicing Buddhist or anyone of Islamic faith.

My parents were always at odds over Daddy's being saved. On

sporadic Sunday mornings Mom would announce over breakfast, "Donna Jene and I are going to Sunday school." My brothers would exchange glances. Mother would invariably direct her next line to my father as she casually raised her cup of tea to her lips, "Do you want to go with us?"

This identical drama would unfold every few weeks, and each of my parents had their lines down pat. Daddy would briefly look over the top of his *Wichita Falls Times* and *Record News* Sunday edition to make eye contact with Mother. "Maybe next time," he'd respond meekly, a cigarette dangling between his lips. This was Mother's cue to get up from the table and remark coolly, "Well, it's you that's going to hell, not me. And not my kids if I can help it."

Soon after this well-rehearsed exchange, I'd don my best dress and Sunday shoes and off we'd go to church. Mom was meticulous regarding my church clothes. My Sunday-only shoes were kept like new, though they usually rubbed a blister, and I often wore puffy nylon dresses in an array of bright colors to complete my attire. She and I shopped at the Ben Franklin store thirteen miles away in preparation for my Christian education each year, but she was also a good seamstress and worked for weeks to make me dresses. I still hold my mom responsible for my shopping addiction, as some of our best times together involved shopping.

Unlike most of our neighbors who were members at one church or the other, Mother would try on different churches like outfits in a dressing room. I never really felt at home in any church because she would eventually find something she didn't like about the pastor or the service and that one would be nixed from her list. We'd then get a reprieve for several months without going to church, even a year would go by, while she decided on another place of worship. The only way I knew she'd found a new church was suddenly finding myself in the middle of the Sunday morning breakfast melodrama again. Her pious announcement, my dad's disinterest, my frilly dress and blistered feet.

Mother had told each of us repeatedly that unless you are baptized before you turn twelve years old, you'd go to hell if you had the misfortune to die after that age. I dreaded turning twelve. But I did eventually reach my twelfth birthday, which meant Daddy and I were now in the same predicament. Neither of my brothers were baptized, so the only person in our household officially slated for heaven was Mother.

My mother never missed an opportunity to admonish my father for not setting the example and "leading the kids the way to heaven." Every summer held the promise of a change in our spiritually stateless status because Vacation Bible School was popular in our little town. The best families' children always attended two weeks of Bible school. The most pious mothers were helpers. Mother insisted I participate. I always enjoyed any kind of school—and the chance to see my friends— so I did not mind going.

In Mother's eyes, somehow my attendance at Bible school kept me safe from Satan. She would brag to my relatives, especially her own family members, how much I knew about Jesus. "Donna was one of the best students in Bible school again," she would write to her mother. Sometimes Grandmother Mattie would write back; sometimes I suspect she just prayed for us all. Grandmother Mattie was extremely devout, and I'm certain that this annual news alleviated her worries about her daughter's brood going to hell.

Being witness to the dichotomy between my heaven-bound mother and my hell-bound father was confusing and terrifying for me as a child. I desperately wanted my father to comply and wondered what he had against Jesus. But even with the ominous twelfth year behind me, I didn't necessarily jump in the righteous water myself either. I hesitated because I wouldn't be able to live a sinless life after my initial swim! I couldn't follow the logic. How could I ever keep from sinning again once I was baptized? No one had explained that baptism was supposed to grant forgiveness for any sin I committed...even those I committed after I turned twelve!

It made more sense to think I would need to be pretty perfect for the rest of my life once I committed myself to God. So I continued to save up my sins and just hoped I wouldn't die in a car accident before I eventually got baptized. I figured Daddy and my brothers were gambling people too—like me, they were saving their sins to be erased when they were dunked. "Do I go now?" I wondered in this spiritual game of Texas Hold 'Em. Or should I wait until I had even more sins to wash away so I wouldn't have as long to be good before going to heaven?

I never felt holy enough for baptism until I turned 21. By then I thought God must have been growing quite disappointed in me and I'd better straighten out. Down I went in the water and was saved. I don't know if I felt better afterward or just more worried that I'd sin again. To tell the truth, I still struggle with what happens if a person sins and doesn't have the opportunity to ask for forgiveness, such as a car accident. I'm missing something that either my mother or any one of the many Christian preachers I met on an odd Sunday morning forgot to explain.

My teenage years were particularly difficult because of my religious upbringing. If I scheduled a date with a boy my mother didn't know, she would compel me to ask him about his religious status. Imagine a fourteen-year-old girl already carrying a load of teenage angst prying into a young man's faith on their first date. Finding a way to insert "Are you saved?" into the conversation was awkward, but I knew Mother expected the question to be answered before the night ended.

If he replied he was not religious, I dreaded reporting my findings. "How was your date?" quickly morphed into her lamenting, "Well, there's another soul probably going to hell." We'd both drop the subject and never revisit it. My mother had done God's duty, issuing a poignant lesson for her heathen daughter. I got her point every time, but I still wanted to know what happened to the person who can't ask for forgiveness.

Mother may not have passed on her religious bent to her children, but I know I inherited my determination from her. If she wanted something or someone to do something, all us kids knew just to appease her by doing it. She was absolutely relentless.

While in college, I visited my parents one Sunday afternoon. I was saved but still secretly perplexed by my questions. Nine hours of religion classes at the university had done little to inform me of the answers. I wheeled in the driveway, wondering what Mother was doing sitting on the front porch. Sitting in the rocker (or any chair) was not her way. She was busy, always.

She met me at the car, her hands clasped like a child's. "Ask your daddy what he did," she cheerfully ordered. Thinking he might have bought Mother a new car, I looked around the driveway but noticed she was still driving her six-year-old Ford. A new car must be Mother's new mission, I told myself. I knew Daddy would eventually go to the car lot and do her bidding—it was just a matter of time.

Mother walked in the dining room with me, hardly breathing until I could inquire what exactly Daddy had been up to. "Hi, Dad," I offered, setting down my bag beside his chair and giving him a hug. Daddy wasn't a kisser but loved a hug any time. "What's going on?" I asked with growing trepidation.

Before he could answer, Mother interrupted with the enthusiasm of a kid unwrapping gifts at Christmastime. "Your daddy got saved!" She looked like the cat with a canary.

I was surprised but not stunned. "Well, tell me about that," I said, looking straight into Daddy's eyes to give him a chance to respond before Mother jumped in. He started to tell me the story but Mother, dissatisfied, cut him off. "Well, all I can say is that it's about time. Your daddy is getting older. Luckily he hasn't died before asking God to forgive all his sins. Oh, Donna, you should have been there..." She launched into her recollection of the momentous event. She and Daddy had been at a tent revival the previous Friday night. "Daddy went with me," Mother said. I believed this was a miracle in itself. "The wind was blowing hard and it was beginning to rain. The preacher called for anyone to come up front quickly and let God's rain pour over them to cleanse them." She paused for dramatic effect. I looked at Daddy, who was clearly irritated by her exuberance. "I couldn't believe it," she continued. "Your daddy got up and stood in the rain with the preacher. He took Jesus in his heart! Amen!"

At this, Daddy slightly smiled and shook his head as if embarrassed. I told my father how glad I was for him, but none of us ever discussed this episode again. There was no need. Mother was happy and Daddy was saved. All was well in our household. The wind had blown my father to God!

Mother and Dad

MY MOTHER, A ROSE WITH PROTRUDING THORNS, was ever-present in our household. Our family was matriarchal, although we pretended my dad was the boss. At times he would feebly try to take the reins only to be berated by my mom's fiery temper. I have vivid memories of her yelling at him, wallowing in self-pity and telling us how bad our father was. He would retaliate by making fun of her weaknesses in a hushed voice that only we children could hear. Daddy knew she would calm down within a few minutes.

Mom was highly intelligent yet had received a poor education, often missing school to care for her eight siblings or working to support them. She considered her highest achievement her nursing training that she received at the county hospital.

Like most mothers raised in lower class families, she wanted her children to graduate from a "regular college." That meant no community college and no tech schools, but a "real university." She felt cheated by having to work at such a young age, but her parents were working poor. They needed all their older children working or babysitting the younger ones. Having had sporadic schooling herself, she made our education a priority. But a straight-A report card delivered by me or my brothers would often be accompanied with her reminiscing how she was mistreated in life. This dose of guilt dampened any of our feelings of success.

The working poor have many demons and one of the most commonly inherited is their feeling that they were given a bad hand in life. Someone else was always to blame, just as their ancestors had wallowed in self-pity. Alcohol, drugs, and broken relationships often reinforce their lot in life.

My dad's family was higher up the social ladder. They were quick to disapprove of my mother in every way. Although none of my three aunts (Daddy's sisters) were college-educated, they had ample money mostly because of my grandfather's work ethic and success in the ranching and oil business. I suspect that, like my dad, they had high IQs and learned very quickly about the niceties that my grandfather's oil checks allowed them. Semi-annual trips to Neiman Marcus in downtown Dallas and lunch at the famed Zodiac Room was my sum total of what it meant to be rich growing up. I like to think that what little I know about the finer things in life I learned from my aunts.

Daddy's family may have been more refined than my mother's family, but they lacked her family's humor and liveliness. Parlor games were compulsory activities in my dad's family, and each grandchild was expected to excel and win against our cousins, aunts, and uncles. Successive losses at canasta or dominoes quickly landed a child a "he's a little slow" label. Our family games were serious, whether physical or intellectual.

One hot Saturday afternoon my older brother, Lee, forced me to sit and play twenty successive canasta games with him winning all 20 games. I was only about nine years old and cried each time I lost, but I learned a valuable lesson. I didn't give up and on the 21st game I beat him fair and square. He was delighted that his protégé had come so far!

Mother was never invited to compete in any family games. Our games were a blood sport, and admittance to any competition was controlled by the bloodline. To maintain her ego she never asked to play and saved her delight for the times when her children were lauded as precocious players. After defeating Lee in canasta my skills quickly earned me a welcomed entry to the adult world.

Mother had a child (my sister) out of wedlock before she met my dad. My sister was sixteen years older than me so I don't remember her ever living at home. She left at eighteen, I suspect marrying a boyfriend as a means of escape. Her three little ones came quickly thereafter.

Enduring a troubled marriage for as long as I could remember, she often left my nieces and nephews in our family's care. I liked having them there, as it gave me playmates, albeit younger ones. My sister had a penchant for bad romances. These rogues often visited our family's home, and my brothers and I tried to stay out of their way. I often found her assortment of men scary, as I still harbored feelings from the perverted act of a stranger years before.

Mom would interrogate each one, mostly disappointed with their status in life. My mother had assumed the position that if she could marry some money, so could my sister. My sister did have several attributes of success—outstanding good looks, a delightful sense of humor, and street smarts. But being labeled illegitimate, I believe, had formed a hole in her soul. I feel certain she courted severe insecurities alongside her suitors.

One relationship between my sister and a man of Mexican descent turned unusually tense and ugly. After several months she broke off all ties and headed to our home, her refuge. Her story that she relayed that evening sent chills through my mother, who was overly protective of her first child. Nothing my sister did or said was ever unacceptable to Mother.

Just then the home phone rang and Mother answered. It was Tito. (I can't believe I still remember the thug's name.) He demanded to talk to my sister, saying something to her like, "I'm coming to get you. And if your family tries to stop me, I will kill them." We all took the message seriously.

He said he'd be at our door in thirty minutes.

I was stunned by my dad's behavior. With a look of resolve and a determined jaw, he began unloading the closet with weapons we rarely saw. By now I was terrified. I could hear Daddy steadily loading shells in the barrels of the shotguns and saw him deliver my mother a handgun. Mother was cursing and nervous, hysterically stating she would shoot the SOB while my sister stood nearby crying.

Both Lee and Wayne were comfortable handling shotguns and hurriedly went outside to hide in the barn. This was my dad's advice in case things got out of hand in the house or Tito brought his friends to help him out. I still remember the bravery my brothers showed in making sure that our family was safe. I loved both of them deeply and was scared they'd be murdered by these outlaws that night.

The minutes went by quickly until we heard a knock on the front door. Mother had installed me and my nieces and nephew in the middle hall closet, a location she considered the safest area. Everything was silent except Tito's insistent rapping, demanding to see my sister. My mother finally delivered her well-chosen response. "If you don't leave right now," she said, "I will shoot you through the door." She meant it and he knew it. After a few choice curse words, he got back in his car (which was loaded with bad dudes). They drove slowly away. It was dusk and we could see their taillights glowing. The road by our house provided cover for vehicles on the south side. When their car drove over a small hill, for a few dozen feet the car was out of sight. We could hear the engine pause and go silent. We instinctively knew they were casing our house.

The barn provided a better sight line than my parents had inside our home. My brothers ran back from there, informing the family that the intruders were retrieving guns from their car. My brother, Wayne, the gentlest sole of the entire family, reached out for my hand when I ventured out of the closet. "Don't worry," he said in the quietest, kindest voice. "We will all be okay. Lee and I can handle these guys." His words made me more frightened. Tears welled, but I remained silent.

In a hushed tone, my dad did all the talking from that point. He rarely talked, so we all listened intently, even my mother. "If you are very quiet, you can hear them talking," he said. Our ally was carrying their voices over the crest of the hill. We stopped to listen and could hear voices being carried by the wind. These hooligans didn't know that the heavy breeze served as a megaphone broadcasting their intentions.

My dad always had great hearing. "They are saying they are going to scare us," he said, his head bowed. That made me feel a bit safer. At least they hadn't said "kill us." Lee piped up and said, "Daddy, Wayne and I can get the jump on them. The wind is blowing hard enough for us to see exactly where they are." Sure enough, the trusty wind was acting like a lighthouse on the grassy fields. Their every breath of air lit up the end of their cigarettes in a red glow, although they were still out of shotgun range. The wind was our friend, and provided the betrayal that allowed our little family the upper hand. We could see them, but they could not see us. We returned to the closet to hide. My brothers, still bearing their arms, crept out to the barn again. *Bang, bang, bang!* I jumped, and my mother let out a muffled squeal. Who had delivered the shots?

I heard Daddy say, "That's the boys shooting." They'd both shot a few rounds into the ground in front of the intruders as a warning, but no one returned fire. Finally, after several more minutes without issue, the intruders turned out to have little bravado and left, my brothers having taken away what bits the criminals had mustered. Without a hesitant stray in the bunch, they all ran back to their vehicle and took off to the south. We could see their taillights grow dimmer as the distance increased between them and us.

I was so relieved and proud of my family for standing their ground. As long as my brothers were in the family home, I knew I was safe. With little fanfare, we had dinner and assured my sister that she would be okay. She seemed edgy but more at ease. My sister seemed to have learned a lesson. None of her losers thereafter threatened our family, and my brothers stayed even more vigilant about having strangers in our home. I was mad at my sister, though relieved that none of us were harmed. I vowed to myself that I'd never date a loser. The minute he was mean, I was out of there. I'd seen what threats could do! We never heard from the Tito gang again, although it would not be the only time our family home was in danger.

Grandparents

T HE HEAT ON A WEST TEXAS JULY AFTERNOON CAN BE stifling, killing a person's desire to do anything more than sit under a shade tree or lie on a couch trying to catch a breeze. With temperatures upward of 100 degrees and scarce wind, the farms eventually give in to the overbearing sun and everyone heads indoors. I loved to go see my grandparents on those days. They had two swamp coolers and the best front porch for catching any wayward gusts. Grandpa was a fixture on his porch, sitting in his favorite perch—an outdoor rocker with cotton pillows protecting his aging frame.

My favorite chair was to his right, a 1940s-looking metal seat painted pale pink and dubbed "Donna's chair." Uncomfortable at best, at least it was next to Grandpa. I felt like a princess when the two of us chatted on long, hot summer days.

Grandpa would tell me stories of when he was a young cowboy, detailing how hard life was on a working ranch in Henrietta, Texas. Sprinkled among his thoughts were usually memories of the day he met the ranch owner's daughter in a one-room country church where she served as the pianist. Her petite frame and her beautiful playing captured his imagination and fueled dreams of being a gentleman rancher like her dad one day, although his dream had little hope of ever coming true. He was poor and an orphan who was never educated beyond the age of twelve.

The cowboy would eventually learn that the pianist was named Lennie—a young widow who had lost her first husband in a gruesome hay bailer accident that cut his body to shreds. Young Lennie had vowed never to marry again, but this tall blonde man riding a gray mare to and from church snagged her attention one day. The blonde and another cowboy were sitting on the last row of pews. As she pounded the keys, she looked up toward the back of the church at the strangers. After a few weeks of these stolen glances, she told her only sister, Carrie, on the way home, "I'm gonna marry that tall blonde cowboy." Carrie just smiled, having developed a secret crush on the blonde cowboy's friend herself.

The two eventually courted, though rarely and quietly, the penniless ranch hand and the daughter of a wealthy man who was a ranch owner and a doctor. My great-grandfather had strict rules, and fraternizing with the help wasn't allowed. Having some money of her own from her husband's tragic death, Lennie was a bit independent for a 22-year-old in 1899 and did what she pleased. She and Carrie would saddle up the horses and go to the creek to meet the boys for a picnic. Away from their father's eyes, they would meet my grandpa Tom and his friend Claude. A sprawling pecan tree provided cover and a romantic backdrop. My guess is there was no sex but lots of flirting and talking.

After six months of courtship during hot summer afternoons, both couples secretly decided to get married—Tom and Lennie, Carrie and Claude. My future grandparents, great-aunt, and great-uncle. Two women of long bloodlines, doctor's daughters, Henrietta debutantes, and heirs to land that had once belonged to Mexico. Tom and Claude, penniless orphans owning only youthful optimism and boundless dreams of land and cattle on their own ranches. The four bolstered each other's confidence and made a time to meet my great-grandfather and his wife at the ranch house to reveal their plans.

I know little of my great-grandmother, as Lennie rarely spoke of her. She was shadowy to me, but Lennie's dad seemed larger than life—mean and ugly. He drank whiskey, delivered babies, and bought more land by the fistful. His wife raised my grandmother and Aunt Carrie, making sure they went to Stephens College after their country schooling. They were slated to be teachers while they waited to marry well.

Back on the front porch, I listened intently to his recollections. Grandpa's voice would change as he told me of their meeting with the boss, Lennie's father. At five feet and just a hundred pounds, Lennie was the spokesman for the foursome. Grandpa spoke little and said that Claude and Carrie never said a word.

With everyone seated on the front porch, Lennie announced, "I'm marrying Tom." The old doctor gasped and yelled, "You will do no such thing." He pointed to both men and shouted, "Get off my ranch. Today!"

I was scared for my grandparents when I heard this part of the story for the first time. I'd seen many guns in the old ranch houses of my family's friends. I knew old ranchers would use them without hesitation and figured my great-grandpa might do the same. "What happened next?" I asked my grandpa, my eyes wide with suspense.

"Well," Grandpa would begin and continue the story. "Claude and I had a choice and so did your grandma and Carrie. We could yell back or sit silent while Lennie defended us all. We chose to sit still and let him rant." And rant he did.

"If you girls marry this trash," he said, "then you're going with them. You will never come back on my land and never get a penny when I die." With raging anger he slammed the door and left the foursome's future to be decided by star-struck twenty-somethings.

With no good plan in mind, the foursome capriciously decided to go to Oklahoma, get married, and find cowboy jobs on the sprawling Oklahoma Territory. They'd find living quarters and stay together. But southern Oklahoma was known to have wild Indians and the girls were afraid.

Despite their fears, Grandma and Aunt Carrie packed a few of their dresses, which took up lots of room in their steam trunks left over from boarding college. Neither knew how to manage a home, as they had grown up with a cook and housekeeper. Grandpa would laugh at this prospect. He said he and Claude almost starved to death eating the girls' cooking.

Grandma owned a buggy left over from her first marriage. Grandpa and Claude loaded it while keeping their rifles close by in case my great-grandpa got drunk and decided to get his gun. The girls tried to cram all their belongings in that buggy but couldn't begin to carry everything as two young women of their stature had many possessions.

My great-grandmother was not allowed to say goodbye and instead sat in her bedroom crying while her two only daughters packed up their lifetimes. When they closed the screened door and left for the final time, they could hear their mother quietly open her bedroom window. But they were afraid to look back.

Uncle Claude drove the buggy, and the two women sat on top. Grandpa tied Claude's horse to the back of the buggy and he rode his gray mare in front. By nightfall they made it to the Red River and camped on the crimson sand. There were cold biscuits for food and squirrels were plentiful in the pecan trees hovering above. Claude was a good shot. Grandpa said it rained that first night and everything got wet. The women were soaked, sleeping together under blankets. Claude and Tom slept by a campfire long extinguished by the pelting raindrops.

The refugees tried to start another campfire, having little success on the sand. The river had swelled with the overnight rain and they weren't sure how to get across it to the shores of Oklahoma. Lennie and Carrie huddled together and cried, afraid everyone was going to drown.

Grandpa knew his mare could manage the currents, but the buggy had no chance. Everyone and everything would perish under the river's rush. Using questionable judgment, my grandfather decided to take his soon-to-be bride on the mare and ride together across the raging Red. If they made it, Claude and Carrie would wait by the buggy and decide if they wanted to risk it.

He helped Lennie navigate her wet and heavy skirt as he practically threw her behind the saddle. He then straddled the leather, praying silently to a little-known God that his girl wouldn't fall off and drown in the river.

A horse swimming in moving water is dangerous. Grandpa taught me that if the animal's nose goes underwater, he goes crazy while drowning and is unmanageable. Even above the water, a horse's legs are powerfully flailing below the surface to keep afloat. Riders can get caught in the swirl of legs, lose their balance, and succumb to the current.

My grandmother desperately pulled her skirt around her body and held onto Tom's strong back. He kicked the mare's sides, urging her to keep swimming, and pulled the reins toward him, making her keep her nose up. Over what seemed like hours, they systematically moved sideways across the running thread of death. Oklahoma was getting closer by the minute.

"Hold on!" Grandpa kept shouting back to Lennie. Grandma was deathly silent. Finally the mare found muddy clay under her hooves, lurching forward until she reached solid footing. The young couple had made it to Oklahoma! They waved wearily back at Carrie and Claude across the river. They waved back, but they made no move to unhitch the buggy and try to cross the river to meet them on horseback.

The Red River is named for the red clay that forms the river bottom, staining everything it touches. Both Tom and Lennie's skin and clothing were drenched in red as they clung to each other for a few relieved moments. Now what? They'd ride until they found other humans in this wild territory and pray it wouldn't be hostile Indians.

In a couple of miles they spotted smoke. Not knowing if it were that of a friend or foe, and too exhausted to think about the consequences, they went toward it. Luckily it was coming from a small wooden building in the middle of a grove of tall trees. A man outside was skinning two squirrels. Tom and Lennie waved to get his attention, but the man was looking down.

The mare needed rest and the travelers needed food. The man's son offered them hot coffee on an open fire and some beans in a black pot, sharing what was to be their dinner with the two strangers. They told the old man and the boy their story, and the strangers shared their own tale about a momma and two sisters who had died of the fever traveling west. With nowhere else to go, Oklahoma had become their home.

My grandparents stayed overnight, leaving the next morning for a small town up the road called Wauika. Tom thought he could get work there. He didn't know what to do about Carrie and Claude but would figure something out. Claude was always his responsibility and Carrie was always Lennie's. It would stay this way for the rest of their lives. It was a long ride to Wauika. The mare was near exhaustion with both adults on her back by the time they arrived. Lennie had saved money from her first marriage, totaling about $300. She had stashed it in her room back in Henrietta and grabbed it on her way out of her daddy's house.

Grandpa talked to every cowboy they met headed for Texas, asking them to check on Claude and Carrie. After a few weeks of inquiring, they finally heard they were back in Henrietta. Maybe back on the old man's ranch.

Grandpa was determined never to go back to that ranch and fervently hoped Lennie wouldn't want to either. They were soon married by a country preacher, although Lennie was never sure their marriage was legitimate! So months later they went back to Henrietta to see Carrie and Claude. They all went to Jacksboro, Texas, in Jack County and got married again, this time by an ordained minister. Lennie was pregnant and felt relieved that a Texas minister had made sure they were on solid matrimonial ground.

Grandpa took some of Lennie's money and bought 59 acres of good sandy Oklahoma soil. The property had a two-room house. He farmed while she mostly read books, including the Bible. "I cooked. Your grandma was always worthless in the kitchen," my grandpa would tell me, chuckling to himself.

Challenges came in waves for the struggling couple. My grandmother cried a lot and missed her sister. Their first son was born and died shortly thereafter of fever. My grandmother could often spot Indians lurking around their property. She was terrified of them and hated Oklahoma. Grandpa regretted taking her away from her big, beautiful house in Texas and separating her from her family. To remedy the situation he made a deal to trade their Oklahoma plot for forty acres in Montage County Texas near Henrietta. Lennie was thrilled. After a year she and Tom were going back to Texas.

The seasoned travelers had acquired another horse and buggy by that time and knew how to cross the river on a wooden bridge. They took what few possessions they had to their new Texas home. This fateful move changed their lives—and mine. The land they had purchased was good farmland with lots of water. Grandpa planted crops, and Lennie made friends with their nearest neighbor—the landowner's wife who lived about a mile away. They owned ten thousand acres of Texas ranch land and lived in a beautiful big home. Lennie felt at home there, visiting the rancher's wife almost daily. They often ate dinner at the big house with the ranching couple. The lady of the house seemed to know that Grandpa was way beneath Lennie's social strata, but she and her husband respected their determination to make a life for themselves together.

Grandpa soon picked up extra work on the big ranch. They lived a decent life, but it was not enough for either of them as they were young and ambitious.

While tilling the soil or herding a cow, Grandpa could still hear the old man saying, "You'll never get a penny from me." He desperately wanted to show him he could make a good living for his daughter, maybe even better than he had done. A few years later, a landman looking for oil approached the owner about drilling on his property. Grandpa's little forty-acre patch just happened to have a big creek on the back side. The oil company needed water to drill and the creek was always flowing.

Grandpa made a deal with the oil company, providing water for a fee. The wells were successful and so they kept drilling. Eventually they leased about thirty acres of Grandpa's land, and our family got our first oil well. Ten years and five children later, those forty acres had proven their worth. My grandparents had enough money to buy three hundred acres even closer to Henrietta with a big three-story ranch house. Grandpa bought Lennie furniture from fine stores in Wichita, and she ordered lace curtains from the Montgomery Ward catalog. They were actual ranchers after just twelve years of marriage.

Grandpa kept buying up land around Clay and Montague counties. He never sold another acre. His goal was to accumulate more than the eight thousand acres the old man had. And he did acquire more. They struck oil on some of the properties, and the day finally came when Lennie could live how she grew up. They had a cook named Frances and a maid named Maude. Lennie read her books and raised the family, making sure the kids did well in school.

After being away fourteen years, Lennie wanted to return to Henrietta to see her family. She wrote her parents and told them when to expect her and her family. As my grandparents entered the metal gate of the old man's ranch house, it looked different than it had years earlier. For the first time in Lennie's life it needed painting and was in general disrepair. As they approached the home, they could see the old man waiting on the front porch.

He didn't speak to my grandfather and barely acknowledged Lennie, although he did say a few words to his grandchildren. Lennie's mother looked a hundred years old. She sat down on the porch with Lennie, talking to her in hushed tones. She mostly cried. Grandpa made sure he told the old man how big their ranches were. He just scowled in return. "It felt good," my grandpa would always tell me, "but not as good as I thought it would." The old man was broken and often drunk in his old age. They never saw him again.

Lennie went to both of her parents' funerals a few years later. Carrie went with her. Claude never acquired property but ended up working for Tom. He never saw Carrie's parents and had no desire to do so. Despite their differences in wealth, Lennie made sure Carrie dressed like a lady. Carrie and Claude had nine children, and Tom and Lennie gave them money often, especially Lennie.

"Donna Jene," Grandpa told me a hundred times recounting this part of the story, "I wouldn't have a penny if I let your Grandma Lennie take care of our money. She'd give it all away to anyone who'd ask." Neither of them knew what a philanthropist meant, but they were each one in their own way.

Grandpa also bought a lot of ranch land east of Wauika, Oklahoma. Throughout his life he kept up with the men he knew from his younger days. They would call him on the old black phone in the hallway and let him know each time some rancher or farmer had died and the land was for sale. We went to his Oklahoma ranch sometimes. My uncle Noah, Grandpa's son-in-law, often checked on the Oklahoma property for him. Noah was the last cowboy of the family. He had a horse trailer and left early many mornings to cross over the border and ride the Oklahoma prairie.

Grandpa never hit oil in Oklahoma. He always claimed Oklahoma was a bad omen for him.

If I acted out in any way, or cried around him (which was rare), he'd look at me sternly and say what was probably the worst thing he could think of: "Donna Jene, you are really lucky. You could have been born in Oklahoma." I didn't know exactly what he meant, but I would shut up immediately, thinking that God might punish me and send me to Oklahoma. I'm so glad I'm a Texan. Any time I fly or drive through our neighboring state to the north, I remember his words and Grandma's admonishment: "Tom, perish the thought!"

Oil Well

ANYTIME A FAMILY MEMBER CALLED ME "GRANDPA'S favorite," I secretly hoped it was true, as I adored my grandfather. I was particularly pleased when anyone in my family would declare how much I looked like Grandpa's side of the family. To me that reinforced that I was wrought from the tall blondes, not the petite dark-haired side of our family tree. Grandpa's family was allegedly German, and my grandmother's English, so I studied both provinces of my purported ancestry voraciously.

Being the baby of the baby of the entire family, my grandparents Tom and Lennie were in their sixties when I was born. With only one other granddaughter and a string of boys between my cousin Betty and me, they were delighted when I, their last grandchild, turned out to be a fair-haired cherub.

Grandma appointed herself my teacher and relished her role as such. Having taught school as a very young woman before she married my grandfather, Grandma Lennie loved books, especially poetry. I was expected to memorize entire poems and to read early. By three years old I could complete nursery rhymes and read words. Grandma took great pride in my accomplishments, and I was content to gain her approval.

Grandpa saw me as his business and ranching sidekick. I would sit very still in his red pick-up and listen to his stories about how Grandma had taken a chance on a young cowboy orphan. As he put it, God smiled on his hard work and put oil in the dirt.

Gulf Oil found Grandpa...and his oil.

The monthly oil checks made life fairly comfortable for Lennie, Tom, and their four children. Their fifth child, my Aunt Lorene, died of tuberculosis before I was born after a stay in the sanitarium. She left her only son, Tommy, with my grandparents, who raised him for several years before his father's sister took him to be with her.

I grew up observing the intricate process of bringing the oil underneath to the surface of the earth. Anytime a new well spouted black gold, my grandpa had a big barbecue right on the land next to the well. Neighbors came in old pick-ups, and other oilmen in big Cadillacs. Some of the men thought they'd get work tending to the wells. Women chatted with Grandma while more affluent men slapped my grandpa on the back, congratulating him on another victory in the oil and gas world. Thank God for Texas!

Gulf kept drilling, and we kept praying for more oil. Watching a rig go up was always thrilling for the family. My dad and mom would drive out to the rig site, hoping for an increase in the family budget. The workers had different names and job descriptions—pipe men, roustabouts, roughnecks, drillers, and pumpers. I was always confused as to who did what but knew they all worked hard with their oil-soaked coveralls and grimy hands.

I was sleeping in my southwest-facing bedroom one morning when my mother woke me in a loud voice, saying we were driving out to the new oilrig. "Why now?" I wanted to know and sleepily rubbed my eyes.

Mother was impatient with my slowness. "Your grandma called and said there's been an accident on the derrick."

I had no idea what that meant, but I bolted out of bed and tumbled into the pick-up with Mother and Daddy. I soon learned the dangers of working in the oil patch.

The rig was about four miles from our house. As we topped the hill near the contraption, we could see only flames. The rickety derrick had caught fire and flames were shooting upward into the sky. The sight was exciting and horrifying at the same time.

We pulled the pick-up as close to the scene as was safe to do. Men were standing all around, shaking their heads. Grandpa seemed to be too close to the fire. I was worried for his safety.

Mom and I stayed in the truck, and Daddy went to Grandpa. I could see him listening intently to his father. After a short while, Daddy came back to tell us a man working on the rig was blown off when the rig exploded. He was burned badly and was on the way to Henrietta General Hospital. "He may have to go to Fort Worth to the burn center," Daddy said matter-of-factly. I knew anyone who went to a big town hospital like Fort Worth had to be seriously injured.

Oil and gas fires are difficult to extinguish because of the ready source of fuel to keep the flames fed. Fire needs air to stay alive, and the Texas wind obliged this need, blowing hard across the barren acres of land. Sudden gusts teased the flames and sent them even higher into the sky.

The fire burned for several days unchallenged until Gulf Oil sent specialists to put it out. Grandpa went out often to see the damage. The neighbors would stop, shaking their heads as if to say, "What a pity that Tom's rig is burning."

I thought God must have gotten mad about something and was punishing us. After all, my grandpa was "saved," but Daddy wasn't when I was a child. My mom used the debacle as another opportunity to poke at my dad's irreligious status. "You're the only child in Grandpa's family that isn't saved," she pointed out. "All our luck may change if you don't follow the Lord." Daddy had ignored her. But not for too much longer.

Fire

MY FIRST MEMORY TOOK PLACE WHEN I WAS JUST three years old. Of course my senses could only make simple distinctions between what was warm and good versus what brought me discomfort. Our home was always something that provided a strong and lasting sense of comfort to me even at such a young age. But one day something threatened that peace and nearly destroyed us as a family.

With three stories, our house seemed impossibly huge to a tiny girl and yet strikingly familiar all the same. Mother kept it spotless and inviting. Built in the early 1900s by a successful oil family, it had tall open windows that allowed the wind to slightly blow the lace curtains my grandmother had hung. Grandpa and Grandma had originally lived there before us, but when they got older they moved closer to town in case they needed a doctor.

I was allowed unlimited access to play with my dolls anywhere I wanted on the first two floors, except in my brothers' bedroom. My brother Wayne didn't know the word "no" when it came to me. But my older brother, Lee, was harsher and forbade me entrance. Mother supported Lee's wishes, so my dolls never got to see what teenage boys' quarters were like. The third floor was off limits to all the kids. Mother used it for storage and a spare bedroom if we had family or friends stay over. My brothers told me that a ghost lived up there, so I carefully avoided even walking by the stairwell leading to the third-floor entrance.

As the youngest girl in both my immediate and extended family, I always had scads of toys. My mother was a superb seamstress and kept my dozens of dolls in fine attire. The dolls lived throughout the big house. Rarely did I place all of them in my doll buggy, as it was often too crammed with their cousins.

My first memory of the morning our lives would change forever began like any other morning. I slept in a small bed in my mother's bedroom. I loved sleeping so near my parents. I felt safe even in the big house with the wind blowing incessantly through the soaring windows and making strange night sounds.

Mother was always the early riser, followed by Dad and then me. To this day I have always looked forward to rising early, anxious to welcome life's experiences for each day. Rubbing my eyes from sleep, I remember stumbling into the kitchen, the first step in my morning routine. Daddy had taken his usual seat at the table drinking coffee and reading his beloved newspaper. Mom typically cooked oatmeal, fried bacon, and baked biscuits. She was efficient and capable at almost anything, including making good breakfasts. I sat down, anticipating my oatmeal made just like I still like it: a spoonful of honey, a taste of butter, and a chipped-up biscuit in the same bowl as the grain. A little white milk poured into the porridge made it perfect.

My brothers shared an upstairs bedroom on the southeast side of the house. They were not at breakfast yet because they never got out of bed until after Mom yelled and threatened them with whatever punishment came to mind each day.

Sitting patiently at the table, Daddy and I waited for the biscuits to finish browning. Mother reentered the kitchen after yelling up the stairwell toward the boys' room. She reached for a hot pad to remove the bread from the oven. I remember feeling a little blast of heat, as the kitchen was already hot from the day's early sun—an omen of what was about to happen to all of us.

As she put the pan on the hot pad, she jumped when a loud explosion and a crackle pierced the air. We looked at each other. "What was that?" Mother asked. Daddy looked puzzled.

"Go check on the boys," Mother demanded of my dad. "They're probably wrestling and broke something."

Usually Daddy reacted in slow motion when summoned by any of us. He despised leaving his passion, reading. But on this day he complied easily, his own curiosity urging him to move faster than usual and investigate the odd noise. He hastily sat down his coffee cup, folded the paper, and left to go upstairs.

Daddy was gone only a few seconds before he said in a loud voice, "There's smoke coming from the third floor!" Mother ran out the kitchen door and I trailed her up the staircase. Even a three-year-old could see danger seeping through the cracks of the third-floor hall door that was always closed off.

"My God! The boys!" Mother shouted. "Get them up. This wind could burn the house down on all of us!"

Daddy ran up the first flight of stairs, flinging open the boys' bedroom door. Why she'd commanded him to go when she took off right behind him I did not know. "Get up, both of you! The house is on fire!" she yelled when she reached their room.

My groggy brothers realized instantly how serious this was. They were ranching kids who had seen plenty of grass fires and knew too well the destruction a fire can cause. As was always the case, Mother had now taken full command of the family, barking orders. We all complied, knowing she was usually right.

"Wayne, grab Donna Jene and both of you get away from the house. Stand out by the water tank. Lee, help your daddy and me. We'll get buckets and you grab the water hose in the front flower beds."

By now the upstairs crackled like a bunch of firecrackers and black smoke billowed through every crevice. I can still see my daddy trying to open the third-floor door as the flames lapped toward him. Instinctively he jerked his hand away from danger.

"We can't save the upstairs," he shouted. "Try to grab the things you want downstairs."

It was so rare to hear my father raise his voice, indicating that the danger had escalated. Always loving and dutiful, my brother Wayne firmly guided me through the back hallway toward the rear door as Mother had said to do. Passing by Mother's bedroom, I saw my doll buggy filled with my cherished playmates.

"I want my dolls," I screamed and tried to loosen his grasp on my arm to go get them.

"Not now," he said firmly and held my hand tighter in his. "Mother will get them for you," he consoled me and I unquestionably believed him.

Daddy told Mother that the nearest fire station was about twenty miles east of our house—too far to be of any help. An east-west paved road took travelers and locals either to Wichita Falls to the west or somewhere to the east. Since we never drove more than fifteen miles east of our house to one of my grandfather's farms, I had no idea what other geography lay in that direction. Daddy and my grandpa would sometimes go to East Texas, but I couldn't imagine where that was! Sixty years ago, fire engines were mostly for townspeople anyway. Country people had to depend on their neighbors for help with fires, accidents, snakebites, storms, or whatever other emergencies came up. Any immediate help we'd get that day would have to come from them, not the fire station.

With the house now an inferno and flames shooting from the roof against the morning sky, our neighbors heard the noise, smelled the smoke, and saw the blaze. Ready to help, they loaded their families in their farm trucks along with buckets, hoses, and blankets to smother the ensuing grass fires. No one was above doing whatever they could to help—women in house dresses, kids still in their pajamas, and farmers in old work boots.

Setting out from their homes, they didn't know exactly where the fire demon was, so they drove in the general direction of the flames. Finding our burning house, they sped through our iron gate. I watched the men jump out with pails in hand as they ran to the horse tank for water. They were fully aware that out-of-control fires on this

West Texas prairie were a danger to every home, acre, and animal. The few watering holes dotting the land would provide a weak barrier to the rolling walls of death. Everyone had the same goal—help your neighbor and help yourself.

The fire, fed by the roaring wind gusts, had engulfed our home and soon burned it down to the concrete foundation. Looking at the rubble, I could make out the charred metal wheels of my doll buggy, but not one of my beloved dolls.

The farmers had successfully contained the flames to just our property. Eventually giving in to the hundreds of buckets of water doused on it, the remnants smoldered—too hot for anyone to search for valuables. They had extinguished the potential killer, but they knew that this fire would not be the last.

Mother cried, I cried for my dolls, and my brothers fidgeted. In the country, men-boys don't cry. My dad addressed the devastation with a seldom-used curse word, a rare display of his emotions. Mother tried to comfort us all, while at the same time proving her unwavering faith in the fact that "it must have been God's will."

The men who had fought the fire could hardly bear to look at the site, as their children stared at the ashes. The neighboring farm women slowly and timidly approached my mother, hugging her lightly while the men patted my dad's shoulder. After chatting quietly among themselves, they loaded up their families one by one and slowly drove out of the gate. I was too little to wonder what anyone was thinking, but I'm sure the mothers were thanking God for their own salvation even while they said a prayer for my family.

The popping noises had all but subsided later that day, and the lingering smoke had blown away with a final push from the wind. We had nothing left but the clothes on our bodies. I learned a lesson about pride when the farm vehicles started reentering our gate. Instead of carrying empty buckets, this time the women got out of the pickups with armfuls of blankets and homemade quilts. They brought bags of groceries, hand-me-down clothes, and a few dishes, providing us with the necessities to carry on living.

My mother's heart was broken and her soul bent. Years later I would hear several of my mother's friends tell me, "Your mother never got over the fire. It took all your family pictures. She doesn't have any photos of you kids when you were little." Family pictures were priceless in decades past, even though their importance is hard to understand in today's world of storing pictures in the cloud. With our pictures gone, memories were lost forever—never to be replaced.

But instead of showing anger and disappointment, my mother graciously received the items offered from our neighbors' big hearts and thanked her community for their concern and generosity. I quietly cried, as no one had thought to bring me a doll. The neighbors had little to give, but they seemed happy to do what they could. Desperation leaves no room for pride and we welcomed their gifts, which we loaded into our pick-up and Mother's car. These acts of kindness remained with our family the rest of our lives. That night we went to stay with my grandparents.

My three-year-old psyche demanded little to be satisfied, despite the traumatic events of the morning. Going to my grandparents was always a treat. I knew they both thought I was the greatest little girl who ever lived—no question! My grandmother always had loads of children's books and plenty of time to read to me. This night would be no different. After she read me a fairytale, I told her how I missed my dolls. She assured me that we would go to town and buy me two dolls, whichever ones I wanted, first thing in the morning. She gently explained that my other dolls had gone to heaven, assuaging my disappointment.

How I loved my Grandmother's south bedroom. The wind entered the open windows and blew warmly over my body to soothe me as we talked together. I sleepily asked Grandma before I gave in to rest, "Mother said ... the wind ... it caused the fire."

"No, honey," she said softly and waited a moment before continuing. "The wind was just doing its job, blowing." After she knew I was falling asleep, she left and went to the living room. I heard the muffled voices of my parents and grandparents talking long into the night that evening.

We stayed with my grandparents for several weeks after the fire. One day when the boys got home from school, my mother made an announcement to all of us, Daddy was standing nearby, silently communicating his approval. "Your grandpa has bought some more land, and it has a house on it. He said we could live there. It's a good house. I know you'll like it." That was that. Grandpa had provided once more as he always did. Mother took charge and Daddy complied.

Later that night, instead of Grandma reading to me at bedtime, Mother lay down beside me. "Donna Jene," she told me, "in the new house, you're going to have your own bedroom."

Suddenly remembering the ghost that lived upstairs on the third floor, I was slightly afraid of this news. "Is it upstairs?" I asked with trepidation.

"No, it is downstairs on the southwest side of the house," Mom replied. I knew nothing about a compass or directions, so I asked her where that was before I felt confident that it was far enough away from the ghost.

She smiled, sensing my fear, and answered, "The same side of the house when you slept in our bedroom at the old house. You'll like it. It has big windows, and the cool breeze will blow right through your room."

Mother could always make any situation sound like an adventure. At least I would never be too hot again! The fire had not extinguished her optimistic attitude. To her, there was always something good to come out of something bad. Time would tell if her theory would prove right.

Keeping Warm in a Cold Wind

OUR HOUSE BURNED IN THE INDIAN SUMMER OF West Texas—late September, early October. A few weeks later in November, the cold north winds made their annual entrance into Texas via the Red River—the dirty, winding river that serves as a border between Texas and Oklahoma. Since we were only a few miles from the Oklahoma border, we always received the first winter wind long before other parts of Texas did.

My mother, the powerful yet kind and loving matriarch of our family, primarily spoke in declarations. Whatever she announced we knew to take as fact. The first time she saw the new house our grandparents had given us, she declared, "This house is not insulated well." My brothers and I were baffled, not knowing what kind of flaw she'd so quickly identified. She pointed to the front door and windows and said to no one in particular, "Those north winds are blowing under the door and the windowsills. It's gonna be a cold winter until your daddy does something to keep the wind out." Daddy looked helpless.

Mom had the family plan to address this problem already mapped out. Without waiting for my daddy to speak up, she said she was promptly going to Wichita Falls to buy electric blankets for all the beds. This made my oldest brother joke, "Then tell Donna she can't wet the bed or she'll be electrocuted." The two boys collapsed in laughter as Mother shooed them away. But I knew what they meant, and I spent the next few nights in sheer panic, afraid of having a mishap. If I did, I might be fried like the man Daddy told us about who had stuck a piece of metal in an outlet and burned all the hair off his head.

Each night became a mental struggle between me and the cold winds. Did I turn on the electric blanket and flirt with an early death, or lie freezing, listening to the wind blowing against my windows and making whistling noises? In desperation I would inevitably choose to stay warm and hope to avoid any electric currents zapping me in the night.

Our new dining room was the prettiest room in the house, but it too was treacherous that winter, given its three northern windows adjacent to the table where we ate. I can still feel the wind seeping under the windowsills, chilling the unlucky person relegated to sit on that side. We children were all aware of the perils of sitting by these windows. At every meal both my brothers raced to secure chairs on the opposite side, trying to stave off the chill. But being the whiny baby girl, one of them always ended up forfeiting a prime spot to me.

During our raucous dinners, only my feet suffered the swirling effects of the north winds as they searched out a warm place inside that icy room.

Christmas Eve was always special to us—and the first Christmas in our new home would be no exception. There was no school that day and mother had busied herself making the best homemade fudge and pralines. As usual she'd wrapped gifts for weeks ahead of time, and we had many packages (mostly cheap, but always one expensive one) under the tree. She coded the names so we didn't know who got what or else we'd have shaken them so hard whatever was inside would break.

That Christmas morning the cold north winds outplayed us. We couldn't sit in the living room where Mother had stationed the Christmas tree because that room had no insulation and the floor was absolutely frigid. My younger brother had to carry every present from the tree to the dining room, which now had a space heater. Just to irritate his little sister, he kept bringing others' gifts and telling me I had none that year, summoning my tears once again.

We were so happy when the winds grew warmer in the year, signaling that spring was on the way. But that season brought its own set of challenges as well. Our former big house with its soaring ceilings had been designed to capture cool breezes. So it took time to get used to a home built with signature 1950s features like lower ceilings and smaller doors, trapping the warm air inside. We would have to depend on air conditioning—something Texans affectionately called the "swamp cooler"—to keep cool in summer. My parents went to Wichita (we always dropped the Falls) and bought our first swamp cooler. Daddy proudly installed it himself on the screened-in back porch, but it only blew air in the kitchen, having little to no effect throughout the rest of the house.

Every time any of the kids complained of the horrendous West Texas heat, the standard answer from my mother was, "Open the windows and get some wind." She didn't allow complaining, so we would shut up quickly while opening the windows and hoping for quick relief. How we prayed for cool breezes every summer.

Although I had the best bedroom location to keep cool at night, I'd recently turned four after we moved into our new home and was now made to sleep alone for the first time. This rite of passage caused me great angst. We lived several miles from the nearest human but within howling distance of every furry night creature. I was certain the wolves that sometimes ate our baby calves were peering through my open windows, watching my innocent figure sleeping. The skunks didn't shy from announcing their visits either. We'd even seen some coyotes at our fence on the south side of our yard nearest my bedroom! Like my conundrum with my electric blanket, I once more fought a no-win situation. Close the windows and bar the wind from coming in and I would surely have a heat stroke. Or leave them open and sleep lightly, hoping to fend off any creature seeking a late-night snack. I loved my room during the daylight and hated going in there after seven o'clock every night when I knew the evening sparring match with my imagination would begin. But I dared not say anything to any of my family. They would all make fun of me. After all, the country is not a place for sissies, even four-year-old girls!

Poodle Skirt

DADDY FIXED THE HOUSE PER MOTHER'S instructions. He installed new insulation, sheet rock, paint, and window caulking. This family would show the cruel West Texas wind something. Now that we could live there in comfort, Mom was pleased with the results and everyone was content.

I was especially happy because we lived about three miles from my cherished grandparents. Being the youngest of the cousins, I was a later-in-life baby. The closest cousin in age was about thirteen years older than me. Betty, my only girl cousin, was twenty years older, so there was no competition for anyone's attention there. Besides, she lived in Houston, which was akin to living in a foreign country in my mind. My other four male cousins lived close by, and I thought they looked just like American Bandstand competitors.

My cousin Tommy let me ride in his Chevrolet convertible with the top down one time. My mother had put my hair in a ponytail that morning, but as Tommy and I drove off (way too fast, I think) the wind played with my ponytail and the rubber band slipped off. I was so disappointed. I had never seen Tuesday Weld's or Connie Francis's ponytails come undone on television. I was afraid that I'd never ride in a convertible again. But as a teenager I had boyfriends with convertibles, so I did!

The summer before I started school, my grandmother and mother had an unspoken disagreement. I knew something was wrong because silent tension began mounting. Grandma Lennie rarely weighed in on our family matters, but being educated, she considered herself an expert at all things school-related. As a young child I loved to read and write, especially poetry. I'm convinced now that my grandmother exaggerated my skills, but she never let me see anything but her delight. I couldn't wait to go to school. The summer months were clicking by and I'd mark off each day with my No. 2 leaded pencil on our calendar as I looked forward to school starting again.

Although I was to be in the first grade with most of my Sunday school friends, my grandmother insisted I was too precocious for my peers and should be immediately elevated to the second grade, but Mother was against this idea. Even so, Grandma insisted that she go with my mother to meet with Mrs. Ryan, the first-grade teacher. Our school was very small and Mrs. Ryan taught both the first and second grades in the same classroom. Grandma pointed out on the way to their meeting that if I studied second grade material, I'd still be in the same room with my friends. I was relieved by this proposition and hoped Mother might agree.

Grandma, dressed in a hat and gloves, and Mother, bareheaded with clenched knuckles, prepared to square off in front of Mrs. Ryan that morning. The three women sat together—Mrs. Ryan at her desk and Grandma and Mother seated in chairs in front. I sat nearby.

"Donna Jene has been reading since she was three," my grandmother said, pridefully launching her first salvo. "First-grade primers will not challenge her."

Then, wanting to prove her point, she looked at me and said, "Come here and read for Mrs. Ryan."

Quickly glancing up at these three women, I realized I was helpless in the hands of these sparring partners. I got out of my seat to obey my grandmother, but Mother had had enough of her meddling in my future.

"Sit down, Donna Jene," Mother commanded. "We need to talk to Mrs. Ryan some more."

I feared my mother's hand more than my grandmother's wishes and immediately sat back down at the little school desk I had been assigned during the meeting.

Mrs. Ryan took a deep breath and spoke next. Looking directly at my grandmother she said, "I don't doubt you have prepared her well and that she can easily do the first-grade work." Before Grandmother could smile a self-satisfied smile, Mrs. Ryan continued. "However, being the same age in years and a grade ahead in school does sometimes pose difficult social problems for a student. They can be bullied and made fun of. The first-graders will taunt them, and the second-graders won't accept them. I recommend that she stay in the first grade."

Unhappy with Mrs. Ryan's dire prediction about her granddaughter, Grandmother rose in a huff and prepared to leave. Mother faintly smiled at Mrs. Ryan and gathered her things. I wasn't sure who had won this round, but I knew it would not be long before a final decision was reached. That night Mother told my father emphatically to let Grandma know that my mother would take care of my education and she should stay out of her family's business. Daddy looked scared but shook his head compliantly.

The next day my mother announced to our family that I would start first-grade. Contented that I'd be with my friends, I was excited to take the next step with Mother—planning my school wardrobe. We broke out the catalogues and began flipping through the pages, and I saw a pretty pink full skirt. I begged for this pink skirt with a poodle embroidered on it. Poodle skirts were all the rage in 1957 and it was all the world to me, so I continued whining to my mother for some time. I can't believe how she let me carry on that way to no avail. Whining was not allowed when I became a mother to my sons, even though I certainly did my fair share of it when I was younger.

My savior was my beloved grandfather. I could ask him for anything, and the answer was almost always "yes." I kept vigil for my poodle skirt all summer. One hot Sunday afternoon at their house after lunch, my grandfather reached in his pocket and pulled out a wad of money. I held my breath as I counted $8.00—just enough to have my pink poodle skirt made by the local seamstress. I was overjoyed. So was he!

Unbeknown to me, my legs were chubby as a child. I still fight this malady. My ex-husband liked to say that women with big legs came from the working class. I'm not sure if this is an insult or compliment! On my first day of school, I was to ride the bus. My blouse with a white round collar carefully tucked in my new poodle skirt. I waited at the bus stop and dutifully held my lunch pail filled with a peanut butter and jelly sandwich and various other goodies. Mother always made sure we never were hungry, thus my chubby legs. In my other hand were my school supplies neatly stacked in my zipped bag, as there were no backpacks then.

When the bus pulled up I made my way to the first step to meet the driver when an unexpected wind gust blew my poodle skirt right over my head! I dropped my lunch pail and my supplies, trying to fight the wind and push down my skirt. What was supposed to be my first day of school was starting out as a total disaster. The redheaded freckled-faced boy from the farm a few miles away started chanting, "What happened, Chubby? What happened, Chubby?" Others chimed in as I felt my face flush and tears begin to brim. I have never forgotten how cruel kids (and grown-ups) can be. Pride can be erased in an instant—if by nothing else, then by good old Mother Nature. If the war is between you and the wind, the wind usually wins. I learned the hard way to be prepared nowadays and keep one hand ready to anchor any loose clothing!

Storytelling

I WAS A GOOD STUDENT. MY PERSONAL PRIDE AND MY mother's expectations (not to mention those of my brothers and dad) served as great motivators for my studious nature. From the first grade all the way through high school, I gladly offered my papers to anyone who wanted to copy them. I was and am still a bit of a sucker for bleeding hearts—a trait I shared with my mother. Having grown up poor, she was generous at every occasion. Her view was that she was darn lucky to have married someone with a little money and she was happy to share it. If anybody asked her for a favor, it was a done deal. Although looking back perhaps her motivation may have sometimes been so that they would be indebted to her.

I also love nerds—always have and always will. I get teased by my friend Diane, who is quick to point out my penchant for brainy types. To me looks are fleeting, but intelligence and knowledge are to be revered in any person. Nothing excites me more that to discuss poetry or a book, and I readily admit that this requires some nerdiness. I have dated some nerds in my lifetime, but never enough.

My dreams have become my intent as I grow older. Namely, I want to host dinners like the famous Dorothy Parker, whose roundtable gatherings of New York's finest critics, authors, actors are legendary. I want to invite intellectuals and artists—the best of the best at whatever each person pursues: chefs, oenophiles, writers, designers, architects, builders, ranchers, politicians, entrepreneurs, and the list goes on.

Since I was a very young woman, my mind has eagerly been preparing for these discussions.

I've envisioned every detail of the table setting, the candles flickering after burning for hours during lively discussion and debate. Good food, good wine, and hard liquor are welcome. Cigarettes only outside and quickly extinguished. Everyone participating at their level of comfort. I often discuss these dinners with the one woman who has my heart—my pseudo-sister, Betty Jean—she continuously helps add to our list of invitees.

Did I mention I came from a family of storytellers?

My family members (each and every one) were good at telling stories, and some were even better at listening, laughing, and adding to the fun. My dad could weave a tale that always brought a hearty laugh and lent itself to our adding to it and embellishing here and there. My mom could be counted on to interrupt if Daddy left out any part she deemed important.

We would all opine in various ways, and if you were really good at it, my brothers would ask you questions just to keep the story alive. In the spirit of camaraderie, there was never any competition among storytellers or putdowns if anyone happened to throw in an errant detail.

Stories might pop up anywhere, as all our gatherings were impromptu. Mom and Dad didn't read child psychology books advising them on how to conduct a family story hour. They just raised a family. I miss so much the story times we all spent together—Daddy and Wayne on the couch, Lee on the matching chair. Me and Mom on chairs we had pulled in from the dining room. All the grandkids, including my boys, joined in the fun—as well as cousins, uncles, friends, and anyone else who wanted to join in. We would stay up late into the night, dreading the clock's passing hours. When I reluctantly went to bed, I did so while envying those who could keep their eyes open for even more.

We loved all kinds of yarns—Westerns, ranching stories, oil and gas ventures, politics, economics, travel, people we knew, sports— nothing was off limits. From presidents to local dignitaries, all were fair game. Of course our family or friends always came out on top.

I hope my sons tell stories with their families like my parents did with us. Stories have served to bond people throughout history. No communication is as effective as seeing another's eyes and smile. Dorothy Parker's roundtables at NYC's Algonquin Hotel are still legendary, not because the participants tweeted each other or posted on Facebook, but because they engaged with each other personally, therefore bonding in their respective passions. Despite popular culture's insistence to the contrary, electronics and cell phones just don't serve the same convivial settings.

Thugs and Hoodlums

SOMETIMES IT SEEMS THAT CERTAIN HOUSES HAVE THE kind of karma that leads to tragedies. By the time my grandparents' home burned, the big house had seen plenty of bad times.

Although I was very young and have sketchy memories of living there, there is one vivid picture of being in that home that I can replay at will. Seeing Mother yelling at strangers in our yard still looms in my psyche. My grandmother was beside her, pushing furniture against the dining room doors that lead directly outside. The person (or people, I wasn't sure then) on the other side was screaming, "We're gonna kill you!"

I stood in awe of the spectacle unfolding before me. "Why do they want to kill us?" I wanted to know, not comprehending what could be threatening us on the other side of those doors. My recollection ends with that scene, but I've heard my family tell and retell the story enough times throughout my life to fill in the details.

Since my grandfather was considered a successful rancher and oilman, our family members, neighboring farmers, and sometimes even perfect strangers constantly approached him for loans. Sometimes when I sat with him on the front porch, as was our routine, I'd see an unfamiliar car or truck pull up the driveway. Someone (usually a man) would emerge and walk up to the porch to talk with Grandpa, inevitably about money. Shaking their hand in a firm grasp, Grandpa always asked the person to have a seat. He never dismissed me from these conversations, and I listened intently to the ensuing hard luck story. Most of the time, Grandpa would give at least a portion of whatever they asked, but sometimes he just said he couldn't do what the person wanted. A powerful person can unknowingly make enemies and pay a price for his or her success.

My family loved card games. The big house was perfect for parlor games. The living room adjoining our dining room was large with double hung windows that opened wide, allowing the wind to blow through to the hallway and cool the entire south side of the house. Various aunts, uncles, cousins, and friends would start an impromptu game often lasting until 1:00 in the morning or later.

On this particular Saturday evening when the hoodlums threatened us at our home, the family card game went late as usual. Dad, Grandpa, Uncle Noah, and Aunt Lois were engrossed in the action. Grandma and my mother were looking on as they sat in the adjoining room at the dining table, dishes from supper still scattered about. I was curled up asleep on the settee, given the late hour. My brothers and cousin

Tommy were sleeping on the screened porch in the back of the house. Suddenly loud shouting interrupted our serene evening as men beat on the French doors just feet away from Mother and Grandma Lennie. A single gunshot rang out, followed by many more. Mother froze, and the card players dropped their hands.

A man standing outside yelled between gunshots, "You tight ol' son of a bitch! We're going to hurt your family!" Gunshots again and a vehicle revving its engine in the driveway. Someone else continued pushing hard on the dining room doors, trying to force them open.

In the country where I grew up, strangers were most often welcomed. They were usually distant relatives or friends of friends. Occasionally people we didn't even know came to Grandpa's door looking for directions since our house was so close to the desolate highway. Had the perpetrators acted civilly, my family might have invited them in. But these people were undoubtedly foes, not friends, and they wanted to either scare us or kill us. No question.

Realizing we were under attack, Mother grabbed a shotgun out of the hall and yelled for Daddy to get the rest of the guns stored in the hall closet. Grandma started stacking chairs against the dining room doors to keep the enemy at bay. Instinctively, Mother then ran to the back porch and gathered the boys without caring what intruder might await her there. Her children were more important than any consideration for her safety, and she herded the boys into the dining room.

Mother, holding the shotgun, screamed, "I'll shoot you through this door! Get away from our house!" I didn't cry. I must have sensed she didn't have time for me. Suddenly the house grew eerily quiet. The men stopped shouting. Mom peered out a window and got a glimpse of a pick-up truck speeding out of the driveway, several men hunched down in the bed of the truck firing their shotguns into the sky.

Grandpa ventured out into the hallway to use the house phone to call the sheriff. So many tragedies happen in the country that somebody making a threat doesn't usually rouse law enforcement. The sheriff was nonplussed and said that if anything else happened, call him back.

That night we all slept—or tried to—in my grandparents' downstairs bedroom. Boys on the floor, me in Grandma's bed, Grandma and Mother with me. Grandpa and Daddy sat up in rockers, Daddy cradling a rifle and Grandpa a shotgun.

The next morning my grandmother was in tears, exhausted from a sleepless night. Mom sat in the kitchen with her jaw tensed. My Aunt Lois was trying to console my grandmother between sips from a hot beer she'd not so covertly hidden in her bra the night before. The 12-ounce bulge was rather obvious on her otherwise thin frame, but what was she to do? She could not walk around with a purse indoors to nurse her habit.

Daddy and Grandpa began looking for evidence of the hoodlums having been in our yard. Grandpa spotted a note clipped to the clothesline. "Give us $100,000 or we will kidnap and kill one of your family," was the ominous message written in two or three variations of penciled scribble. Grandpa tucked the note into his shirt pocket, walked into the house, and again called the county sheriff.

While they waited for the sheriff to arrive, Daddy and Grandpa gave instructions to my brothers and Tommy. Tommy was my grandfather's favorite grandson and looked very much like Grandpa. "You boys stay together and stay around the house. No playing in the barn or in the pasture until we catch these guys." Mother said I had to be with her every minute. I couldn't even play in my room alone. The windows that usually stayed open most of the time so the strong breezes could blow through the house remained tightly closed and the house was stifling hot. Open windows might have made it easier to kidnap one of us.

It wasn't long before a black-and-white painted car with a big whip antenna that was almost longer than the car was wide pulled into our driveway. The sheriff had a big belly, a gun strapped to each side of it, and a sweat-ringed Western hat. His deputy was skinny and nervous, as if he wished he was somewhere else. They walked toward the porch and Grandpa asked them to take a seat.

This was my first encounter with a law officer, and I was relieved they were with our family. Seeing men with handguns was new to me, as I'd only seen rifles and shotguns within handy reach to kill rattlesnakes and sometimes a coyote around the ranch.

Grandpa handed the sheriff the wrinkled note taken off the clothesline. The sheriff looked at it briefly, then looked my grandfather in the eye and spoke. "Looks like you made somebody awfully mad, Tom. Do you have any idea who this might be?"

My grandfather shook his head and said nobody'd ever asked him for $100,000.

The sheriff grunted. He answered, "Well, I guess they think you love your bunch, or they'd have asked for less." At this my grandmother started crying again.

Mother brought the two men some iced tea and we all sat silently. "Have you checked the barn?" the lawman inquired. My grandpa's homestead had several barns, and a very large one would be an ideal spot for the hoodlums to hide. It had a loft that we kids loved to play in and several horse stalls on the main floor. In the summer the horses slept in the pasture, as the barn was usually too hot inside.

"Darrel, go down there and check out the big barn," the sheriff demanded of his deputy. Darrel looked ashen. He looked at Daddy and silently pleaded to have backup in case he found the criminals. Daddy didn't offer to go. Dismayed, Darrel started walking slowly toward the potential hiding place.

The sheriff told Grandpa that there wasn't much they could do, other than driving down our road occasionally to check things out. He warned us to be careful and just wait to see if these guys left another note. Again the same advice—if they come by again, call him.

Darrel returned from the barn looking much healthier than when he'd entered it. Nothing there. He joined his boss and they hurriedly drove out of the driveway, gravel popping under their tires. Grandpa said resolutely to the family, "The sheriff isn't going to be much help. We're gonna have to be careful and try to catch these guys ourselves."

Several times during the following months, the thugs left threatening notes demanding payment either on the clothesline or on the windshield of one of our cars. Our family lived in fear, clinging to each other and to our guns. Mother grew increasingly frantic that one of her children would be snatched away from her. Grandpa even hired a man to go to school with my brothers and wait in the schoolyard all day. I was never out of my parents' sight.

The intruders eventually became bolder. They would leave dead birds around the grounds and once put poison in our horse water tank, killing Grandpa's favorite mare. My grandmother begged Grandpa to give them the money, terrified that something was going to happen to her family next.

"Lennie, if I give them the money, they'll never stop. We will always be in danger," Grandpa explained. "We have to stand up for ourselves." Grandma would cry again each time he refused her. All the women were scared to death for their children's sake.

Daddy and Grandpa hatched a creative plan to put explosives in one of our older cars! When the kidnappers approached to leave another note on the windshield, Daddy would detonate the car bomb. Against my grandmother's will, they ran wire to the car, parking it fairly close to the house.

The plan didn't work, as the thugs either saw the wire that night or they were surveilling our house during the day when Daddy was stringing the wire. Daddy, my uncles, and Grandpa had waited by the windows all night, guns loaded. Sure enough, the criminals came by, but instead of approaching the car, they blew up our mailbox. Things were getting more dangerous and tense.

The next morning my Grandpa called the sheriff a third time. Blowing up the mailbox changed things in our favor. The sheriff told Grandpa that tampering with a mailbox is a federal offense. He would contact the FBI. Two days later the FBI men drove up from Dallas and Daddy and Grandpa met them on the porch. The agents were very calm as they explained that we should remain calm and let them handle the situation from here.

Within two days my grandfather received a call from the FBI men. He and my daddy drove to Wichita, and the women stayed at home, shotguns loaded. In a few hours, Daddy and Grandpa returned and we all ran out outside, anxious to know what was happening.

Grandpa said it was over. The FBI got the men. After questioning them, the FBI discovered that one of the men had met Aunt Lorene in the sanitarium where she spent her last months. She had innocently told him the story of my grandpa and our family's successful oil business in Henrietta. She even told him of her little boy Tommy and how much he looked like my grandfather. When the criminal left the sanitarium, he headed straight for Henrietta hoping to cash in on this information.

The kidnapping and murderous threats were over, but an undercurrent of stress haunted our family throughout my childhood. My mother remained perpetually panicked that there were other hoodlums aware of our family now who wanted to harm her kids. She never trusted strangers again and was overly protective of all of us from then on. We observed strict curfews until we left for college, and I remember constantly having to call to check in whenever we were out with friends. Even with the West Texas wind always blowing, she suffocated all of us.

Travel

I T'S INTERESTING THAT 95% OF US RESIDENTS HAVE traveled to five states or fewer. This statistic by no means includes our family. A big part of our conversation revolved around where we'd like to go next. We would prepare for our trips meticulously, Daddy reading every travel map and point of interest and Mother preparing to pack our meals for the road. These discussions sustained us through boring winters because there was always a summer trip coming up.

We drove, never flew. Flying was never even a consideration. Before my parents bought a camper, which wrapped over the top of our pick-up, we stayed in motels dotted along our chosen route. My dad loved historical monuments and markers. Without hesitation we stopped at every one on the highway we were traveling. Taking a family picture of us beside the icons was a must. Mom was the usual photographer but was most delighted whenever I offered to take her image on these family journeys.

Mother told long stories about her coming from a family of wanderers, her daddy having been a horse trader. She regularly encouraged me and my brothers to go around the world someday. Later when I traveled professionally, I would call Mother to update her on my whereabouts. She'd summon my father wherever he was in the house to let him know that Donna was in China or Chicago. Either place was fine so long as I was safe and enjoying the trip.

She and Daddy continued their trips together after I left home. With great pride and anticipation she'd tell me, "Your daddy and I have decided to go to Little Rock." Or maybe it was Albuquerque, just as long as they could plan a sojourn somewhere. Most of their friends traveled little, rarely left Texas, and certainly went no farther than Oklahoma.

Colorado in the summer was an annual must for our family growing up. We would load up the camper (which we later upgraded to the travel trailer) and head out for Idaho Springs, about fifty miles west of Denver. My grandmother's housekeeper had inherited a cabin there and we used it every August when the heat in Texas was unbearable. I loved waking up next to the raging spring behind the cabin and hearing Daddy getting the fishing poles ready. Lacking the patience for fishing, I'd oblige Daddy by sitting on a rock with my pole dangling half-heartedly in the water. I usually had a book with me, which he heartily approved of.

One summer when I was about fifteen years old, we met some locals in town. Mother invited them for dinner and their tall, good-looking eighteen-year-old son came with them. He was a lineman for the county, apparently making good money for a young and uneducated mountain boy. After dinner he invited me to go up the mountain the next day to check an electrical line on the top of a nearby peak.

My hormones were raging, and his must have been in overdrive. Driving up the narrow road to our destination atop the mountain, we flirted outrageously. About two miles into our journey, he stopped the county-issued truck in the middle of the road and surrounded me with his arms while we kissed passionately. No more than a passionate, romantic interlude. That night I dreamed of being a lineman's wife.

When I told my mother I really liked him, she was furious. "No more time spent with the mountain boy!" she demanded. "You'll get in trouble and he won't be anywhere around." Mother never got over having had a child out of wedlock and was always terrified I might do the same. In true teenage angst I cried and temporarily hated her but soon returned to having crushes on cute Texas boys once we got home from our trip.

Sometimes I'd go on a trip with my best friend Diane's family. We went to Tennessee one summer when I was about thirteen years old in their pull-behind-the-car pop-up camper. Several teenagers went along with us. Diane and I slept in one tent and I got strep throat. I was so sick when the group went to the Grand Ole Opry in Nashville that I remember laying my face on the church pew inside the show. My fever was raging, and I was so mad at myself for causing Diane's mother to have to nurse me. I was mostly afraid they'd never ask me to go traveling with them again!

When my brother Wayne married at eighteen, Mother was so upset. He had graduated high school in May and married my sister-in-law on

June 18. They were young, but we all liked Linda and her family very much. Her brother Homer was four years older than me, and we'd laugh and talk for hours.

The newlyweds planned a honeymoon in Okmulgee, Oklahoma. Wayne already had a job lined up in Okmulgee, and they wanted to go there for a few days before moving their belongings. I am still amazed that they allowed Homer and me to go with them to Okmulgee. We stayed in a rented trailer with me in one bedroom, Homer on the couch, and the newlyweds in the back bedroom. For four days and nights we drove around the state, ate fast food, went to outdoor movie theaters, and even went bowling—just like regular teenagers.

Oklahoma is infamous for sudden storms. One night a strong west wind blew dust and hail through the tiny town of Okmulgee. Our rented mobile home provided little shelter for us and none for my brother's car parked outside. As the wind twisted the tin roofs of some neighboring abodes, hail pelted against the mobile home like gunshots.

Wayne, always the worrier, insisted that Linda and I stay away from the windows. He was certain the wind would break the glass and flying shards would kill us. We were all fully experienced with the damage a twister could do, so we went to the back bedroom and sat on the floor to wait it out. Just teenagers, we felt invincible. I felt so grown up, as for the first time my mother was not there screaming, "Donna Jene, get in the hall closet." The wind blew, the hail spattered, and rain poured, but the entire storm lasted only about twenty minutes. When everything calmed and we felt it was safe to leave our refuge, we ventured outside to survey any potential damage.

Wayne had saved money to purchase a decent car, and he was

proud of it. We were all sick when we saw his vehicle after the storm. It looked as if it had developed a horrid case of acne, huge hail dents on every body part. It was ruined. Money was short for two eighteen-year-olds just starting a new life together. Not concerned with who was watching, my brother cried and cursed the clouds. Linda was ready to go back to Texas. In solemn procession we all quietly packed our suitcases into the dimpled vehicle and drove back to my parent's house—berating Oklahoma under our breath the entire way. Wayne refused the Oklahoma job, never permanently living in that tornado alley.

Mother always kept a little stash of cash saved. Wayne explained what had happened to his car, and I saw her later hand the money to him. Although it wasn't enough to restore the 1958 Chevy's luster, he knew by this simple act that she loved him enough to want to help him.

Two years later, Wayne was living in Texas and working for Texaco Oil. He bought my sister-in-law a new 1965 Impala. By then the young couple had a sweet little two-bedroom ranch home—with a carport that would protect the Impala from future hailstorms! They felt safe.

For years after, during sporadic storytelling, one of us would occasionally mention the Oklahoma storm and remind each other of Wayne's misfortune of attempting to move there. We would let out a collective sigh and our unanimous agreement that Oklahoma was far too unlucky for our family. We were Texans—our birthright was never to be questioned.

Mother's Illness

UNLIKE TODAY'S MODERN WOMEN, 1950S HOUSEWIVES often wore dresses while doing household chores. My mother usually wore a cotton shirtdress. One hot summer day the southerly winds whipped the bundle of clean clothes she was attempting to pin to the clothesline. In vain she kept trying to hold the ends of her skirt down while lifting her arms to complete her task.

I loved the smell of newly washed laundry whenever she delivered it fresh from the wires stretched between two poles. The sun and the wind were perfect laundry detergents. Sometimes I would go out to the clothesline and hang a few of my things myself. I suppose I liked the idea of handling my own clothes. But boredom would soon overtake me and Mother would say, "Go back and play. I've got this."

Content to leave the rest with her, I would happily comply and go on my way.

But this day was different. I asked to hang some of my clothes, and she looked at me with tears rimming her eyes. Rarely had I ever seen my mother cry.

"What's wrong?" I asked, having no idea what could possibly bring my strong mother to tears. The wind again whipped her skirt and snapped the clothes hanging by pins. "You need to learn how to do everything I do in the house," she told me, not looking my way as she finished pinning a dark skirt to the wire. "Okay," I hesitatingly replied with a questioning look on my face. "But why, Mom?"

She directed her watery gaze on me. "I went to the doctor again today," she said. I knew she'd been having some pain in her abdomen. "Donna Jene, I have cancer."

I threw my arms around her waist and hugged her, having no idea if she'd be dead within days. This was my first experience with cancer. I'd heard my grandmother sometimes say that some old lady she knew had died of cancer, and as a ten-year-old girl I assumed this malady only happened to old people. Not to a woman my mother's age. My mother couldn't have cancer—she danced with me when we put 45 RPM records on the player, we went on all-day Saturday shopping trips, and she never seemed tired.

Pondering what my mother had told me, I wondered, "What happens now?"

She silently hung the rest of the basket of clothes, and this time I helped her until we finished. I remember how heavy my brothers' wet blue jeans felt as I tried to make the clothespins hold them while the wind played a violent tug of war.

That weekend Mother packed a small bag for the hospital. She was to have surgery the next Tuesday. For some strange reason Daddy didn't hug her or show any affection. He sat silently. The house seemed solemn. I felt as if maybe my mother had contracted a deadly plague. I wasn't sure if I could catch cancer like a cold, so I made sure I didn't drink after her.

She instructed me that if anything happened to her, I would stay with my brothers and Daddy. My grandparents would also be there for me. I loved my grandma and grandpa but instinctively knew that everything would be different—and for the worse—without Mother, the spirit and personality of our home, everything would drastically change.

On Tuesday, the day of my mother's surgery, my brothers and I went to school as usual. We planned to go to the hospital at 3:30, not knowing what to expect. When school let out my aunt drove us the twelve miles west to the hospital in Henrietta where I'd been born.

"Is she okay?" my brother Wayne wanted to know as soon as he walked into the hospital and met Daddy in the lobby. Wayne, as was his tendency, was overcome with worry. Lee and I were more stoic. "She made it," my daddy offered. "But, they don't know if they got it all."

My mind raced...Who is *they* and what is *it*? Whatever "it" was, it sounded bad.

I went into Mother's room with Daddy. Her skin looked pale and very much like what I thought a dead person looked like. Growing up in Southern Baptist country, I commonly attended funerals with my grandparents or my mom and dad. It was customary for everyone at the funeral to hug or at least touch the corpse residing in the casket. Death was a part of the circle of life. Funerals served as family reunions and always concluded in a jovial feast of covered dishes and casseroles. I loved parties, and for country people, funerals provided the perfect Christian opportunity to get together.

I also knew that Christians believe a person is better off dead only if he or she was saved. I was certain that my mother was saved. She had reminded us regularly of this fact during our childhood, ever chastising my dad for his negligence.

Looking at my mother that day in the hospital bed, I decided that if she died, Daddy and I would go to the First Baptist Church and get baptized right away. If my strong and determined mother could die, God could call any of us home any time he wanted to. We had to have insurance just in case, I told myself.

Having had a tough surgery, Mom recovered in the hospital for ten days. I learned later that the surgeon had removed seven malignant tumors residing in her abdomen. The significant blood loss made her so weak. I only got to see her three times in the hospital, as she didn't want our homework to suffer. She made sure our routines were followed despite the situation. In our home, schooling always took precedent over anything else. This event would prove no exception.

She finally came home from the hospital on a Sunday. Daddy carefully wheeled into the driveway, as my mother was precious cargo in the front seat. Never one to offer assistance before, I was surprised to see Daddy carrying Mother's suitcase. This worried me, as up until that time my mom was always the self-sufficient warrior, even when wounded. Daddy was the compliant yet incompetent follower. With this role reversal playing out before my eyes, I was certain that we'd soon be summoned to her bedside to be informed of Mother's impending death.

Daddy settled her in bed in her room and I was very quiet while she slept. Wayne, Lee, and I sat in the front room together. Wayne whispered, "Do you think Momma will die?" Lee, irritated by Wayne's worry, retorted, "I guess she'll tell us when she wakes up." Lee was never one to show much empathy.

She did eventually wake up and sure enough we all went into her bedroom to see her and await her news. In a soft voice she said, "Okay, you kids. You are going to have to take care of your daddy." We glanced at each other and knew then that she must be dying. She took another slow breath. "I have to go to Houston in about six weeks when I'm strong enough to travel," she said. "I am staying there three months and will have treatments every day. They are not sure they got it all."

Again, I thought, who is *they* and what is *it*? This time I asked. "The doctor is not sure I'm cured of cancer," Mother explained. "The hospital in Houston is going to give me chemotherapy to try to get rid of anything that might still be in my body."

By now Wayne was crying. "Momma, are you all right?" he managed to ask between sobs. She smiled faintly and said, "I don't know."

Proud of her nurse's training, Mother always loved to talk about any ailment or disease. This episode of her own medical treatment was no different. For weeks we heard blow-by-blow the details of her surgery, her recovery, and what to expect at MD Anderson, the famed cancer hospital in Houston where Mother would stay.

My mother in her favorite outfit—the martyr—rather enjoyed having her pity party. I loved my mother very much but despised her tendency for hypochondria and martyrdom. Because she wore any sickness, aches, or pains like a badge, the rest of us rarely complained unless we were bedfast. Mom was always sick enough for all of us.

Our phone was tied to a party line, with three other families sharing a single line. When we all grew tired of hearing her recount stories about her cancer, Mom would keep the phone line busy with calls to all the relatives and any friends who would listen. If a relative happened to answer, she would recite another detailed description of her surgery and how she "might not make it" when she went to Houston. This, followed by assurances that she "is brave" and needs "no help." Mother would have to go alone, she would remind them, as her kids had school.

Again, Mother never considered traveling by airplane, and she refused to drive in such a big city. She would ride the train to Houston, rent an apartment by the month, and take taxis whenever she needed transportation. When she was well enough to travel, Daddy and I drove her across the border so she could board the train in Waurika, Oklahoma, bound for Houston. Daddy and I drove back to Texas without a word. I looked out the window and wondered if and when I'd see Mother again.

The house seemed so empty without her. Words were sparse and Daddy seemed more lost by the day. We went to my grandmother's home to spend each night. I hardly remember staying at our house throughout the six weeks my mother was in Houston. Grandma and Maude, the cook, took over our daily lives, and Daddy gladly let them. Nothing pleased my grandmother more than to supervise my homework, harkening back to the days when she had been a schoolteacher before marrying my grandfather. She loved poetry, and we often read together. I still love the imagery of a poem, thanks to her.

On Sunday nights Mom would call our family long distance to touch base. As the weeks went by I realized that my school term would end before she could come home. I asked my father if I could visit Mother while she was in Houston. This was a big decision for our family, but it seemed logical to a child. I insisted I could ride the train just as she had done. What could go wrong?

My grandmother was absolutely against the idea and Daddy, never wanting to defy my grandmother, kept his usual silence. Mother must have been terribly lonely for some company because she decided that I could make the trip after all, if she planned every detail. Daddy would put me on the train in Wauika bound for Houston. I was to take a lunch and snacks and be sure to remember to potty before getting on the train. Only in dire circumstances was I to move from my seat. Mother even let Daddy buy me a *MAD* magazine to read on the trip with its silly word games and stories. I felt like a grown woman of ten years old.

The train took about five hours to make its way to Houston. I hardly moved and virtually memorized the entertainment magazine cover to cover. When the train wheeled into the Houston station, I saw many tracks converging and several other trains pulling in at the same time. What if Mother couldn't pick me up? The station was so big that she might lose sight of my train in the commotion. I told myself I could just ask an older, kind-looking lady seated near me how to get to my mom's apartment somewhere near the hospital. That was the entirety of a ten-year-old's plan, but it helped to calm my fears.

Thankfully my mom was standing near the tracks, ready to grab me when I stepped off the train. She smiled with a look of relief when our eyes met. Her little girl had made it safely there. Mother took me to a little café and bought me a sandwich and ice cream. I had done it, gone across the entire state of Texas all by myself. True to my family's love of travel, Mom was once more the trailblazer and cheerleader. She never wanted any of us to miss a chance to experience something new. For all her ailments, perceived and real, I love her to this day for cultivating this spirit of adventure in her children.

Migrants

M OST OF THE LAND IN WEST TEXAS IS WORN AND dusty, making it better for cattle ranching than for growing crops. This truth was ideal for my father, had he had a choice in the matter. Daddy was always more motivated to read a book than to drive a tractor, and cows are far easier to raise than cotton. Cotton farming is dirty and sweaty work. But when Grandpa, who owned the land that my daddy would inherit, declared that 80 acres of it should be planted in cotton, Daddy complied. The only son of a successful oilman, Daddy must have resented this 80-acre patch of effort. He would have much preferred anything to meeting the demands of sun-parched cotton fields that would take up all his time.

Every season Daddy would hire a local man with a tractor to plant cottonseed. Then we'd wait for rain to nourish the sandy soil. I'm not sure how he was introduced to the Mexican migrant family that lived in a short bed truck. But one hot and sultry summer June day the truck was parked in our front driveway. Mom and I had just returned from grocery shopping and getting the requisite ice cream cone from the Dairy King in Henrietta.

Daddy was smoking his Camel straight cigarettes and chatting with a short dark-skinned man in a hat and a dirty, wrinkled work shirt. Their conversation looked serious, so without hesitation Mother interrupted. She usually handled most of the business discussions, as she felt that Dad was a pushover. She ordered me to put up the groceries in the house. A half-gallon of ice cream didn't last long in the hot wind blowing through the open kitchen windows.

Thirty minutes passed and the wiry Mexican man started his old truck. It took a minute to fire up and let out a bellowing backfire as he slowly backed out of our graveled road.

"Who was that and what happened?" I was quick to question. Mother typically did Dad's talking and answered, "That Mexican family is going to work the cotton crop. Your daddy sure doesn't want to do it." This was to be my first encounter with Mexican migrants. It became a lesson in life that would stay with me to today.

Daddy added that the man would return with workers next week. They would use hoes to dig up all the weeds sprouting around the fledgling cotton stalks. Weeds were the enemy and could quickly overrun the weak cotton seedlings. Only the laziest of farmers let the weeds win the land. Daddy may not have had any love for farming, but he would not be labeled the lazy son of a rancher. I didn't think another thought about this little man and the dilapidated truck, never suspecting that the sight of it would soon become an integral part of our little 80-acre cotton patch.

The next week I saw the truck pull into in our driveway and loudly lurch forward before the motor died. The little man from the prior week hopped out, smiling through half-broken and stained teeth. I ran to get Daddy. "The Mexicans are here," I yelled. I knew Daddy would be pleased. He had his books and papers spread around his leather chair, and their arrival meant he'd have far less disturbances from reading his pages that he so loved to do.

I went to the front door with Daddy, curious about how many workers the man had delivered. I assumed I'd see a bunch of men like the highway workers Mom and I saw on the way to Henrietta. I was stunned by my view of a working migrant family.

For the first time I noticed that the back of the man's truck had no door but was only covered by a flapping sheet blowing in the wind. The tiny man barely reached the covering, but he appeared to be very proud to display his home for us to see. Inside the back were two shy teenage Mexican boys, two teenage girls about my age, and an older lady holding a tiny brown baby.

The cloth covering now free of its clamps, heat inside the truck bed hurled out toward us. The older woman appeared to be fixing a meal. She seemed surprised that Daddy and I were staring at the ordinariness of her task and looked away, either shy or embarrassed.

The teenagers were as curious about me as I was about them. With little in common but our age, we sneaked peeks at each other. The girls smiled at me, the tall Texan farm girl, and me at them. The boys quickly jumped off the truck bed as if to get away from our prying into their poverty. I went to bed that night still captivated by this family.

The next morning I looked south to the cotton field to see the old white truck parked on the west fencerow. I was able to make out five of the family members scattered among the south end of the field, backs bent over, working. I wondered where the sixth member was.

Daddy walked in about that time and asked if I'd like to ride down to the field. I agreed to go.

Ordinarily I never went to any field. My family liked to tease me about being a displaced city girl. They were so right. I detested everything about the country, except the occasional solitude that allowed me the quiet I wanted for reading and writing poetry.

When we pulled up next to the truck, the older woman was rocking the crying baby. She looked at us briefly and then turned her head away as she had done before. The Mexican daddy approached my father and they chatted for a few minutes. I stayed near the woman in the shade of the truck in total silence. The teenagers would hoe in the cotton field all day under the hot Texas sun.

The rear covering was open and I could now see directly into their home. I spotted a few small stacks of clothes, bedding on the floor, and a few pots and pans in the corner. There were also a few boxes of food and two big water jugs. No television, no fluffy covers on bed frames, no table for homework or meals. This was a life I could not imagine living. I wondered if they moved to a house during the school year, never considering that school attendance was not an option for the teens.

As the two men continued talking, I saw the rest of the family staring at me from the field. We were all embarrassed. Me for feeling guilty about their poverty; they for being poor. Daddy and I eventually went back to the house and Mother asked about the Mexican family. I told her I thought they lived in the truck. She agreed that it must be their permanent home.

The family stayed on our property for two weeks. I learned that Maria and Josephina were respectively fourteen and fifteen years old. I was never sure of the age of the boys. One seemed older than Josephina and the other was a total mystery. I really liked Josephina. She seemed very mature.

I felt sorry for them, as did my mother. Their plight must have reminded her of her younger days struggling through poverty. She seemed determined to make their lives better, though there was little she could do. We cleaned my closet and delivered my used clothing to the girls. I told my mom that I hoped these garments would make good school clothes, still not understanding that they would never go to school. Mother sent Daddy to the truck on missions of mercy several times, once carrying a pot roast with potatoes and carrots and several cakes and pies.

I visited the truck several times and was struck by how attentive Josephina was to the baby. After spending a hard day in the sun, she seemed anxious to relieve her mother of the crying child. As the baby of the family myself, I had absolutely no experience with small children and marveled at Josephina's motherly instincts.

Mother and I often discussed my new Mexican friends. Like her I loved having people visit our home and we invited the girls up for a visit. Late one afternoon Josephina and Maria knocked on our door, walking the half-mile from the field to our home. The hot summer wind was whipping their long brown hair and what appeared to be a white bundle of cloth in Josephina's arms.

I welcomed them inside and they quietly entered our fanciest room, the living room. Mother brought two glasses of iced tea intended for the girls and asked Josephina what was in the cotton cloth. The baby whimpered, surprising both me and my mother. Wondering why the girls brought the baby, Mother asked if their mother was sick.

"Oh no," answered Maria. "Josephina has to take her baby as soon as we get home."

Her baby. Mother and I looked at each other. The baby was Josephina's? A child with a child. Mother reached for the infant, asking if he'd eaten anything. Josephina acted embarrassed and shook her head no. Mother whisked the baby to the kitchen where I supposed she would get the baby some milk or other appropriate food.

Three teenage girls, millions of miles apart in life, stood quietly together in our carpeted parlor. I finally asked Josephina where her husband was. She spoke enough English to know Mother and I were perplexed about her situation.

Josephina said, "I'm not married."

Maria, the more talkative one, continued the revelation of more details. She had gained enough rapport with me and Mother during the two weeks that she felt comfortable sharing Josephina's plight. Josephina stood quietly while Maria told the story.

Josephina had gone to live with their uncle the previous year, leaving behind the family truck that had been her home. She was to keep the small children of several families in a small Mexican village and would be gone for several months. When her family went to visit her, Josephina was already pregnant with the baby. No longer able to care for so many children and carrying embarrassment in her belly, the young girl had rejoined her truck family and given birth months later.

THE WIND BLEW INNOCENT

Josephina, looking sad and scared, quickly gathered the baby in her arms at this point in the story. She made her way to the door and onto our front porch. Maria called after her, but Josephina—afraid of the shame she might meet in our eyes—was headed back to the truck carrying the cotton bundle close to her body.

Maria ran after her, and Mother looked at me to see my reaction. I must have shown my utter shock that such a young girl could be raising a baby. Mother picked up the half-empty iced tea glasses, shook her head, and said, "You don't need to be going to the truck anymore."

A teenaged mother herself, Mother certainly didn't want me tainted by potential sex talk. She probably thought Josephina might tell me how a baby was made, and Mother wasn't ready for her daughter to hear about the birds and the bees.

I heard Mother talking to Daddy in hushed tones later that night. In the typical Southern way of dealing with uncomfortable issues, we never discussed the baby again. Maria and Josephina came through our cotton field two more years after that. I stayed home from then on and looked to the south whenever I saw the old truck parked there. Then one year the old truck stopped bringing the family. Daddy hired a professional man with a machine that picked the cotton for him.

I still think about that family, how hard they worked, and how little future they had despite their efforts. Even now when I hear fortunate Americans criticize illegal aliens, I think of this struggling family and Josephina's baby. I often wonder how her baby was conceived. Years later Mother and I opined that it was probably the uncle's doing. Rapes were and are still common when the sexual predator has all the power. Josephina had none, and sadly she and the precious, hungry baby had to pay the price.

Smokin' Pot or Bananas

OUR FARM WAS THIRTEEN MILES FROM A GROCERY or dry goods store, and even then, the town offered limited supplies of everything. Wal-Mart was still exclusive to Arkansas, and Walgreens was nonexistent in our secluded patch of Texas. Television and magazines saved us from sheer ignorance regarding world events.

In the absence of things to do, my mother allowed me to watch soap operas at a young age. I soaked up images of gorgeous houses where sexy, heartless women flirted with the men du jour on *As the World Turns*. Summers were especially fun because they afforded me free time to watch several of the spicy shows back to back.

Consequently I thought everyone in the big city was rich and glamorous, spending their time drinking wine and having sex during the day. This lifestyle was totally foreign to everyday life on our Christian farm. The seldom-purchased alcohol in our home came in a brown glass bottle. No celebratory corks ever popped in our kitchen.

Sometimes when Daddy watched the nightly news I became mesmerized by brief scenes of sparsely clad teenagers and twenty-somethings marching in New York and San Francisco. They were "hippies," I learned. Having no idea how to get there, I desperately wanted to be one.

Dope and pot seemed to be a requisite to having hip-length straight hair and strumming a guitar. I had access to hippie music on my 45s, but I didn't know anyone with any drugs.

Mother and Daddy occasionally played cards with neighbors, and one of the families had three extra handsome and chatty boys who were a few years older than me. I loved to go to their house, as the younger two boys flirted with me. I felt certain that they could become hippies in the unlikely event that they went off to a college in a city. Watching Ed Sullivan one Sunday night at their home, I sat on the couch with the boys nearby. The Rolling Stones were Ed's guests. As they bellowed out "I Can't Get No Satisfaction," I suddenly felt ever the adult, flirting with one of the boys as much as a little girl could.

Amid our banter, he asked if I'd ever want to try pot. I wasn't sure if he meant cigarettes or if it came in some other form, but I signaled my interest. I casually asked him where to get pot. Like me, he didn't know anyone with drugs. But, he said, he did know how to make something just like pot and we could "get high" on it. I felt my heart racing with adrenaline at the thought. In a hushed voice, he instructed me on drying and crushing banana peels, promising that this would make an ideal substitute for pot. I was frozen with wonder. I was far too chicken to have ever tried drugs if I'd had access to them, but maybe I could make my own.

Mother always bought bananas for our family at the Piggly Wiggly grocery store. The next day I excitedly ate the insides of bananas until I had a mild stomachache and took the peels outside to dry. By tomorrow I'd have the makings of a hallucinogen on my back porch. My cousin was staying with my aunt for a couple of weeks. She was a year younger than me. I called her that afternoon and told her of my impending experiment, and she immediately wanted in on the fun. When I awoke the next morning I crept outside to check on the progress, but the darkened banana peels were still moist. At this rate, I presumed it would take weeks before they would be dry enough to roll into cigarette paper, much less smoke it. I was beyond disappointed that my foray into apostasy had ended so abruptly.

Calling on my mother's determination, I began thinking of alternatives. I told my cousin that maybe a hair dryer was the best way to dry out the peelings. It was much faster than the sunshine and we could probably have substitute marijuana in only a few hours.

I knew to never let my mother catch us in the act, as I'd get either her hand or a belt across the first part of my body that she could reach. We quickly determined that our house was not safe for the unfolding of such a heinous crime. But with my cousin staying at my aunt's big, rambling ranch house for a few weeks, we plotted to carry out our plan there.

I loved my aunt's home. It was three stories with a full basement, a skating rink on the third floor, and ten bedrooms and eleven bathrooms—the epitome of luxury as far as I was concerned. There was also a bomb shelter at the end of a long tunnel and a basement that was perfectly suited for our needs. My aunt rarely went down there and there were dark corners and cubbyholes throughout that could hide our stash of drying peels.

My cousin had a little sister who was a pain for both of us. She would tattle on us for sure, so we waited until she was napping to begin our venture. We opened the big double doors to the basement, armed with my aunt's portable hair dryer—a pink plastic 1960s style, with a bonnet and hose attached. We had difficulty stuffing all the peelings into the bonnet without it collapsing as the bonnet lacked the shape of a human head to keep it properly formed. We stuffed paper around the peelings until the bonnet was so full it sat upright at the end of the hose. We decided that the highest heat setting should render dried bounty in about an hour. My aunt had gone to town and left us alone for a short while, giving her space for a couple of drinks without guilt or interruption and allowing us time to work.

We went back upstairs with the dryer going full blast, pleased that the plan was working so well. The basement doors opened onto the hall leading into my aunt's guest bedroom where we went to await the results. Two open west windows flanked with billowy lace window coverings created a serene atmosphere in the room as the wind gently blew the curtains. My Aunt Lois had inherent taste, and her guest bedroom was stylish and comfortable. I loved that room most of all the rooms in her big house. I never got to sleep there, as whenever I spent the night with her, she would put me in a spare bed on her sleeping porch. Although she called it a porch, it was spacious with three beds and gorgeous wooden floors and floor-to-ceiling windows. The room was always cool, as the window blew from north to south.

We were giggling with sheer delight at our own ingenuity and would have seemed high already to anyone within earshot. I turned on the white transistor radio I'd brought for the occasion and we sang along to the Beatles' "She Loves Me." About twenty minutes into the process, I smelled a whiff of something familiar that reminded me of my dad's cigarettes. I knew it could not be my dad at my aunt's house. I quickly prayed that this scent did not mean another adult was nearby who could be our undoing. Alerting my cousin, we began racing through the house to see who might have entered smoking so we could make sure they didn't discover what was taking place behind the basement doors.

Running through the hall I spotted grey smoke seeping under the basement doors. I flung them open and immediately saw a small flame near the hairdryer. Fire was no stranger on Texas farms. I had seen many and had been schooled on controlling a fire quickly. Instinctively I grabbed my aunt's red embroidered bathroom towels from the guest bath and began snuffing out the flame with the cotton. Miraculously I put the fire out in a few seconds, but heavy smoke lingered.

My cousin, her stricken baby sister standing dumbfounded behind her, panicked. We both knew that little sis didn't have to report us—this darn smoke would announce our sinister activity soon enough. Shaking my head at the disaster that had befallen us, I checked on the hair dryer to survey the damage. It was now a heap of melted plastic. It, along with the paper and a nearby chair, had caught on fire. The flame was gone, but the evidence told the whole story.

I had to get the peelings out of the mess, as I could not think of any way to explain why there would be remnants of bananas in the rubble. I tried to pry out their remains with little success. My only hope was that my aunt would be disgusted by the mess and just toss all of it in the trash without inspecting the contents of the melted heap.

My aunt was a jovial alcoholic and a wonderful woman. She had returned earlier than we expected, possibly from her favorite liquor store. I prayed earnestly that she wouldn't tell my mother about the debacle, even as I privately concocted a scheme that could blame the situation on my aunt's being drunk. When we went upstairs to confess to what had occurred, I saw that my aunt was near collapse as she often was by midafternoon.

She was woozy and didn't seem to understand why we had burned up her hair dryer. "I'll have to go to town tomorrow to get another one," she sighed, silently cherishing the opportunity for another beer run. I said a silent prayer thanking God for her inebriated state.

My cousin and I resumed our cover-up in the basement and removed all the telltale signs— destroying the dryer, its contents, and the towels. The west wind graciously carried the lingering smell of burnt plastic outside through the open windows. Two naughty young girls and their accomplice, the west wind, had all escaped without repercussion. We were lucky that hot Texas summer afternoon— almost too lucky for our own good as we felt we had gotten away with something dastardly.

Mother arrived to pick me up from my aunt's home later that day and my keeper's alcohol-induced nap conveniently buttressed my guilt. Mother's face grew worried as I told her about my aunt's latest mishap, burning up the hairdryer. She just pursed her lips and said, "Your aunt is going to kill herself or you kids. I'm not sure you should be staying with her anymore."

I didn't argue and said very little. I did feel badly about pinning the crime on my aunt, but not enough to take the physical punishment that my mother would have doled out. I took the coward's way and so did my cousin. They say there is camaraderie among criminals, but we were careful to not discuss our near disaster. We simply ignored our failure and never discussed it ever again. The little one didn't know enough to refute our story, so we resigned ourselves to go about our lives without having had the opportunity to smoke fake pot. I was just so relieved that I caught that I didn't grieve my one lost chance to get high.

Daddy, the Pacifist

MY DADDY, THOMAS SHELTON JR., WAS KNOWN TO everyone as T. S. or merely T. These shortened designations were probably more significant and telling than his family realized at the time they gave them to him. Grandpa Tom would always tower over my dad until his death. Daddy was born into what many call "the lucky sperm club" with the right genes that meant there was no pressing need to accomplish much. My grandfather had already been infinitely more successful than Daddy ever could be. Daddy worked alongside my grandpa most of his life, but he had the simpler tasks and shortened hours.

Only once did I overhear Grandpa express disappointment over his only son's lack of achievements. Grandma Lennie immediately scolded him, saying that my dad liked other things instead of tramping around barren pastureland with my grandpa. She appreciated and approved of my dad's affinity for books, undoubtedly attributing this to her own education as a young woman before she was married.

My dad's personality was as truncated as his nickname—a man who said few words and remained aloof to life's pressing problems. He grew up under the protective hand of my grandparents and later had my mother, the controller of all things. The good news is that these stifling circumstances seemed to fit Dad's desires just fine.

Once Grandpa had oil money, my grandmother reverted to her early years of comfort and largesse. She was generous to anyone and everyone—especially my dad. According to my aunt's tales she bankrolled Daddy's early years: new cars, partying and gambling with his friends. Looking back I realize that Daddy was probably ill prepared to marry and certainly to marry a woman with a child.

Mother worked for the general hospital in Bowie, Texas, when my dad was admitted as a car wreck victim. Mother particularly enjoyed telling the story about how when she entered his room and saw the tall, blonde rancher's son, she decided she'd marry him. Daddy had no chance of rebuffing the petite, lively brunette. A few months later, much to the dismay of my grandmother, they eloped to Oklahoma and got married. Many of the engaged couples in Texas crossed the Red River in pursuit of immediate matrimonial bliss because Oklahoma did not have the three-day waiting period required in Texas. My mother's mother kept Mom's little girl while she was gone.

Grandma Lennie never quite forgave my mother for being socially scarred, but for 69 years Mother proved to be Dad's perfect antidote for life's difficulties. She was always prepared for every situation; she liked having control and spoiling Daddy—treating him like one of her patients.

In retelling the story, Mother never left out the fact that when she and Daddy married, he was oblivious to the notion of settling down. He continued to drink and party like his single pals while Mother stayed at home with her child. After a few months of enduring Daddy's boys' nights out, Mom decided that things had to change.

One cold West Texas Saturday evening, midnight hit and Daddy was AWOL. Mother's temper took over. The wind was howling as she gathered my dad's belongings and pitched them in the front yard. In retelling this story she loved to say how the wind scattered Dad's belongings, making them hard for him to recognize in the dark. Dad arrived home very late in a drunken state. Mom had locked the door and pretended to be sleeping. Wearing only a lightweight coat, he was frigid in the wind. She didn't relent to his persistent knocks and yells, keeping the door closed and bolted. Daddy gave up and walked to neighbors about a mile away, where he spent the night. Daddy loved to interject at this point how when he returned the next morning, Mother delivered him a frosty reception both emotionally and physically. Then they'd both laugh; Mother—ever the victor—laughed the loudest. Daddy seemed to delight in all of Mother's victories—even those that came at his expense. I believe this must have been the secret sauce in their long, successful union.

Although Mother had no money, no means of support, and a small child to feed, a drunken man-child was not what she had signed on for. The next morning she packed her suitcase, put some sandwiches in a bag, and drove fifteen miles to Bowie, Texas. The train to Ft. Worth stopped in Bowie, and she was planning to be on it. Her new husband could continue his partying, but she had a child to raise.

Mother bought the ticket and waited pensively in the station. Then Daddy walked in with Grandpa. They came toward Mom, Daddy speaking first. He looked contrite, meekly stating, "If you'll come back, I'll never have another drink." He looked pleading. Grandpa was silent, letting his son pay his comeuppance. Knowing that her future would be very difficult without the help of these two men, Mother reluctantly agreed to try it again. They drove the fifteen miles back to the farm and the home they shared due to my grandfather's generosity.

Both my dad and grandfather now fully understood my mother's true grit. Both having gained a new respect for her, Grandpa developed a close relationship with my mom through the years. If business needed to be conducted involving my nuclear family, Grandpa would include my mother. Daddy was usually the bystander.

True to his promise, Daddy never drank again other than a rare and occasional beer. Then it was only one. If friends or family offered him a drink, Mother would quickly say, "He's not much of a drinker." Dad would shake his head, affirming her statement. My dad had a healthy reverence for Mother but could irritated by her strength and resolve. Her force of personality towered over Dad's. But I always believed that he had made his best choice by marrying my mother. She raised her family largely independent and uninterrupted, leaving Daddy ample opportunities for his favorite pastime—reading his newspapers and books.

Mother's sense of humor and love of fun was very infectious, and Daddy was almost always a happy onlooker. We kids looked to Mother for our daily needs and to Daddy when it was story time. Always ready to comply if we wanted a story, Mother would usually send us to bed only after Daddy had given us a history lesson wrapped in a detailed conversation. We kids all grew up loving history largely due to Dad's lessons.

Like everything else in our home, the family budget was also pretty much controlled by my mom. However, I did see my dad take a stand one hot summer afternoon. Mother and I had been carefully inspecting the latest Sears catalog to select my new school clothes. The 1960s staple came at the beginning of summer so country people could order in time for the first day of school. There were only two seasons for these large tomes of merchandise: a winter edition and a summer one. The winter catalog brought fall clothes and Christmas gifts. The summer one was important for selecting my traditional Easter frock.

Mom and I busied ourselves in the delights of discussing my new winter coat. Should I get red or navy? Short or long? My mother had good style for a poor country girl and a particular sense of color. She dressed stylishly after marrying Daddy and made sure that my closet was overfilled with choices. I must admit that I was spoiled at an early age in this way—too many clothes and shoes.

Mom and I were sitting on our back screened porch filling out the catalog order form when my dad, once more with his head in a book, suddenly and unexpectedly jumped up from his seat. "Follow me," he demanded. Mother and I looked at each other, having no idea what could possibly entice him from his favorite activity, sitting on the porch reading.

He strode through the hallway and into my room, Mom and I following behind him with growing curiosity. Flinging open the door to my closet, he loudly announced, "Donna Jene doesn't need a new winter coat! She has too many clothes already."

I broke into tears, shocked that my father would deny me, his baby girl, without checking with my mother. Mom was the one who denied us, never my father. She looked steely eyed at my dad, silently daring him to utter another word, then breathed heavily and purposefully. "Well," Mother said flatly, "she *will* get a new coat."

I stood motionless, still reeling over having seen my dad's unusual outburst of energy. His issuance of a bona fide opinion in our presence was new terrain. I thought maybe she'd finally pushed him over the line and he'd gone crazy. They stared at each other, each with jaws clenched. I was a spectator, nothing more, in this contest of wills.

Daddy, sensing that World War III was about to begin under his roof in West Texas, quickly resumed being a pacifist. War was too much effort. "Okay," he folded, seemingly exhausted from having almost stood his ground. "Go ahead and order her one." Mother had won again. Game over.

Lee - brother (17), Billy - sister, high school senior
Wayne - brother (14) , Me - first grade

Aunt Faye
and family

Aunt Lois,
Daddy, Aunt Bess

Mother's grandparents

Daddy on the ranch. After two fires, I have few pictures of my parents left.

Grandma Lennie, 90 years old

Daddy and a friend in town

Me (5) at my grandparents' home with my doll

*Brandon (4) telling
Santa a secret*

*Brandon (11) and
Collin (9 months)*

Brandon, an Eagle Scout, 1991

Mom, me, and Brandon - Grapevine High School graduation

Collin and I skiing, Beaver Creek, CO

Brandon and I skiing, Lake Tahoe, NV

*Collin,
Colleyville
Heritage
High School
graduation*

*Collin showing
his new teeth!*

Collin played lots of sports as a child (top, bottom)

Diane, my best friend for 57 years

My best friends of 42 years, Nancy and Ray Farrar

Betty Jean, my dearest confidant, with husband John

Campaigning and enjoying being Colleyville's mayor (top, bottom)

DONNA ARP
MAYOR

Brain Cancer

W HEN GRANDMA LENNIE STARTED SLOWLY GOING
blind due to glaucoma, my grandparents accepted the
inevitable and moved to a small house in a tiny town nearby. They
believed she could better navigate the walls and furnishings in a
limited space instead of the expansive ranch home they had lived in
for many years.

I never missed a chance to hop a three-mile ride to their house.
Sometimes my brothers would take me on their way to somewhere
else, and sometimes Mom or Dad would drive me over there to spend
the day with my grandparents. Grandpa was less inclined to inspect
his ranches as he aged, and I missed the summer days spent in the cab
of his red pick-up, rambling along through miles of pastureland.

Now the lazy hot afternoons were reserved for front porch talks. How I loved sitting quietly reading a book or poetry in his presence. He would interrupt only when he had a story to tell me. "Donna Jene, you wanna hear about..." he would always start, and off we'd go on a verbal journey.

One July afternoon I asked to be dropped off at Grandma's house as usual. (It was never termed Grandpa's house. Home was Grandma's; land was Grandpa's.) When I arrived I immediately noticed that the front porch was empty. That was unusual. Our rocker looked lonely, empty and swaying back and forth in the south wind. I assumed that Grandpa had gone inside to tell his beloved Lennie some tidbit and would soon hear me coming through the front door.

I entered the living room and still no Grandpa. Frances, their aging maid who had been with them many years, gently pulled me to the side. The house was quiet and dark. She said, "Don't bother your grandpa. He's in his bedroom and has a real bad headache." Curious, I tiptoed to his room and silently looked through the doorway. He was lying in his bed with a wet cloth over his forehead. I'd never seen my grandpa in pain.

Seeing his still figure underneath the white sheets and hearing light moaning from his lips burned into my young psyche. I instantly felt that something was seriously wrong. I made my way from his room to sit outside on the front porch, still expecting him to open the screen door anytime to join me. He didn't leave the bedroom that day. Grandma rarely came outside because her limited eyesight kept her confined to her safe environment indoors. So I sat alone watching cars go by. As people are apt to do in a small town, most waved or honked because Grandpa knew everyone and everyone knew him.

My brother picked me up about 6:00 that evening. For the first time in my life I had missed my Grandpa time. The next morning the white wall phone that hung in our hallway rang early. Mother answered and soon announced that Aunt Lois had taken Grandpa to the hospital in nearby Henrietta. Alarmed by this news, I begged Daddy to go see him.

Later in the afternoon, our family made the thirteen-mile drive to the hospital. I was the first inside Grandpa's room. I was disappointed to discover that he was sleeping and unavailable to me once more. We waited until the doctor made his afternoon rounds. He sat with my parents and my aunt, discussing Grandpa's condition. I could not hear what they were saying, so I focused my attention on the body language to decipher what was going on. They spoke in hushed tones, as my aunt dabbed her eyes with a tissue. The doctor patted my aunt's shoulder and shook my dad's hand limply. My mother nodded. Mother then walked across the room to me and Wayne. "The doctor thinks Grandpa has brain cancer," she said. She spoke quietly but matter-of-factly, as a nurse would do when communicating bad news. Mother always had an "it is what it is" attitude.

I didn't cry, remembering that Mother had had cancer a few years before and she was fine now. Surely Grandpa would fare much the same. I might even get to go to Houston again on the train to see him at MD Anderson.

I would soon learn that this cancer was different. The doctor gave Grandpa six months to live, at most. He was in intense pain and remained under heavy sedation much of the time. Not wanting him to wake alone, the family established constant vigils, assigning times for various family members to remain at his side. Although I was just twelve years old, I gladly took my turn with my Aunt Lois. We sat with Grandpa from noon until four every day at the hospital. My mother, brother Wayne and sister in law Linda relieved us when our shift was over.

No longer a child, but hardly a woman yet, I passed these long summer afternoons by reading books and watching beloved soap operas on the black-and-white TV in Grandpa's room. My mother would occasionally bring me magazines that she'd bought at the local pharmacy. Having worked in hospitals, she well knew the stressful boredom families experienced watching their loved one die.

My afternoons were especially lonely because my aunt, her large handbag filled with Schlitz beer cans, continuously visited the ladies room. She reeked of alcohol after 1:00 P.M. By four o'clock she was stammering, making any attempt at lucid conversation with her impossible. The time passed agonizingly slow.

The family was well aware of her drinking but rarely discussed it and just shook their heads whenever someone brought up the unpleasant reality. My aunt was an exceptional businesswoman and the eldest of the siblings. Her unchallenged designation as the executor of my grandfather's estate did not go unnoticed by my parents. They, along with my father's other sisters, wanted to remain in her good graces in case my grandfather died. I actually loved Aunt Lois very much—she had a kind heart and was funny, never mean-spirited, whether she was drinking or not. She was also very bright and money motivated, and my grandfather made a wise choice selecting her as his surrogate.

Grandpa often made noises in bed, flailing his arms and legs, but he was never lucid again until the day he died. We stroked his head often and held his bony fingers. I'm not sure he knew we were there, but I like to think he was aware of our presence.

My aunt was sometimes too drunk to drive and would sleep it off on the couch in the front hospital waiting area. On these occasions I sat with other relatives instead. My sister, a 29-year-old divorcée with three children, was living in Wichita. She occasionally drove to the hospital to visit, gladly sitting with whomever was on duty when she arrived.

One hot summer day Wayne, Mother, and I were sitting with Grandpa when my sister walked in. Boredom overtook her after about thirty minutes in the hospital room, and she invited me to walk to the Dairy King to get a Coke float. I loved Coke floats and was anxious myself to get out of the hospital confines.

It was early evening by then, but the streetlights allowed us to see our way to the Dairy King. In 1963 female carhops were the servers. We sat down at one of the outside wooden tables and my sister asked the carhop to bring us each a float.

A carload of four men pulled up to the speaker near us and bellowed their orders, whistling coyly at the carhop. Then they turned their attention toward us.

"Hey, good looking!" they shouted. My sister smiled and I looked down. Intimidated by their advances, I was sure they were signaling their interest in my older sister.

After some urging from the vehicle's occupants, she told me to stay put and she'd go over and see what these guys wanted. My heart began to beat rapidly, as I felt certain that they didn't want a twelve-year-old girl around.

I was wrong. My sister summoned me to the car and said to get in the back seat. The men had offered her a ride back to the hospital. It was now too dark to walk so I complied, crawling in the two-door car across one man's legs to settle nervously in the middle of the backseat.

The car backed out of the gravel drive away from the speaker and sped onto the pavement. I naively thought we'd be safely back with my mother and brother in a few minutes.

The driver, probably in his mid-twenties, put his arm around my sister's shoulders across the back of the front seat. The men were whooping and talking loudly. Each one had a cigarette and a beer. They offered me a beer and teased me when I refused. My sister drank with them.

I sat silently, my eyes taking in how grown-ups must act when they are out on the town. I was most afraid of being teased by these guys. The driver was named Jerry. He pulled my sister to him and kissed her while speeding the car down the pavement. I knew we were headed toward Wichita, as this was the way my dad drove on the way to the city.

The man-boy to my right started inching his finger around the leg of my short shorts. He was laughing and smoking, blowing smoke toward my face. "Hey, Billie," he shouted to my sister over the wind blowing through the windows, "it's your little sister that got all the looks in the family."

My sister turned her head and smiled. No longer embarrassed, but now increasingly frightened, I knew he was trouble and I was the target. The other boy in the backseat just looked blankly at me.

Driving fast, the car wove erratically on the road while the radio blared. My sister was laughing nervously. I wanted to join in but felt woefully inadequate and unprepared for these adult shenanigans. My backseat occupants were both focused on me.

Suddenly Jerry pulled off the highway and stopped the car. "Boys, let's have some fun," he yelled out, throwing his beer bottle out the window. He opened the door and pulled my sister from her seat, walking toward the dark trees and barbwire fence. I could see him stretch the barbwire for her to cross. She looked back at me but didn't say anything.

I was frozen, my heart beating rapidly. The two boys were discussing whether I should kiss them. The one to my left decided to get out, I think it was to pee or vomit. He was gone a while. The one who was fingering my shorts asked me, "Have you ever had a man?" I whimpered no, unsure of what he meant, but looked him straight in the eye. For some reason he looked scared too.

"Bobby, where the hell are you?" the man shouted around me. No Bobby. It was just the drunk man left in the front seat while Bobby relieved himself in the bushes on the side of the road. My sister was nowhere to be seen.

I could hear the man beside me breathing but didn't know his name. He suddenly let go of my leg and grabbed my face, forcing his tongue in my mouth. I remember that slobbering wet slather to this day. I'd never had sex but I knew his intentions were rough. I was terrified and helpless.

Bobby showed up and had trouble opening the door because of his inebriated state. He slammed down the front seat back so he could crawl in again on my left side. "Jimmy," he said, "leave her alone. She's a kid." So Jimmy was his name.

"Oh come on, you son of a bitch," Jimmy yelled, although Bobby was sitting right next to us. "I'll be gentle."

I didn't move. Bobby said louder, "I said she's a kid." Jimmy stopped spreading his slobber over my mouth and acted disgusted. "Asshole," he glanced at Bobby and got out of his side of the car either for another beer in the trunk or to relieve himself.

Bobby sat silently, as did I. He chugged his beer, never looking at me. Finally he said, "I have a sister about your age. If someone hurt her, I'd kill him." That was his entire conversation with me, but I instantly felt safer. The man in the front seat never turned around but grunted when Bobby said those words. I thought maybe he had a sister too.

Jerry and my sister were soon crawling through the fence and walking toward the car. She quickly looked back at me and asked, "Are you all right?" She seemed anxious and worried. I nodded yes. Bobby said to her, "Don't worry, nothing happened."

Jerry turned around in the narrow lane and headed back to the Henrietta General Hospital, our original destination. He pulled into the parking lot and my sister and I got out. He sped away before we entered the doubled glass doors.

My sister looked at me and said, "Don't tell Momma or we'll both get in trouble." I never did, but I lost something that night: a child's innocence. I never felt safe around an older man again.

She and I walked into Grandpa's room as if nothing had happened. Mother sat in silence while Wayne and Linda ate the sandwiches Mom made every night and brought to the hospital. I swore that my mother sensed something had occurred. She later questioned my sister about where we'd been but never said a word to me. When it came to my sister, Mother preferred a lie over bad news. It was easier for her to allow my sister to spin the truth. I stayed silent, picking up a leftover magazine I'd already read many times. I needed a hiding place for my eyes as I silently considered what I'd just experienced. My daddy and Aunt Bess came at 10:00 that night, prepared to spend the night. We all left, Billie driving back to Wichita and Wayne driving us to the farm.

Grandpa steadily worsened overnight, hardly ever moving any body part. Aunt Lois, sober, picked me up at 11:30 the next morning. I had already eaten, and she had stashed her beers in her bag to carry with her. About 2:15 I was groggy and bleary eyed from reading my newest book for hours on end. Aunt Lois was dozing off in another one of her alcohol-induced snoozes. Grandpa suddenly moved. He tried to sit up but was too riddled with pain and feeding tubes.

I shook my aunt awake. "Aunt Lois, Grandpa is waking up," I said and excitedly tapped her chest. She raised up slightly, looking at him.

"Do you see him? There he is," Grandpa murmured. For the three weeks that he had been in a coma in the hospital, he had never uttered a single word.

"Who, Grandpa?" I cried out, going to him. "Who do you see?"

"Lorene, do you see him?" he demanded again, this time louder and stronger. "He's at the end of my bed."

"Grandpa, it's Donna," I said softly, tears beginning to form in my eyes. "Not Aunt Lorene."

Aunt Lois shamed me lightly. "He believes it's your Aunt Lorene. Let him believe that."

Aunt Lorene, who died at only 22 from tuberculosis, had been sent by my grandparents to a special hospital called a sanatorium in Tucson, Arizona. This place was purported to help her breathing and gain strength. She eventually came home when the Arizona doctors said she was not getting better. Most of my family felt my grandparents' special fondness toward me was due to my uncanny resemblance of Aunt Lorene. Both my grandparents would often remark that Aunt Lorene was the liveliest and most fun of their children. She was a daddy's girl, and it must have been a sign from God that I was such a grandpa's girl. Whenever they would tell me I was "the smitten image" of Aunt Lorene, it made me proud. But I did not want to be mistaken for her now. I wanted my Grandpa to know it was me standing beside his hospital bed.

Grandpa seemed delirious, trying to point his finger toward the end of the bed. "Lorene, who is he?" He excitedly asked over and over, "Can't you see him?"

My aunt had by now regained composure and summoned the nurse. I was frozen to the spot where Grandpa had seen me, or Lorene, or someone else. I would not disappoint him being reunited with his favorite daughter.

He was calm and breathing more shallowly when the nurse entered the room. She looked at both of us and said with startling assurance, "He's leaving us now." She continued, "I've seen this many times. I believe they see Jesus before they die. Jesus has come for him or maybe the Holy Spirit." Then she said the words that as a devoted grandchild I would forever cling to: "Your grandpa is on his way to heaven."

I was so overcome with emotion, I didn't cry. I just kept telling him Lorene is here, Lorene is here. I took his skinny, emaciated hand in mine. The nurse asked me to step aside as she took over with medical necessities.

She announced, "He is dead." Then I cried.

In shock, I whimpered to the nurse, "What do we do?" She hugged me, seeing that Aunt Lois was too woozy to follow instructions, and told me to take my aunt to the phone and call Daddy and Mother. "They will want to know," she said.

Intuitively I knew my life would change. I still wanted both of grandparents to brag on me. I needed them to watch me grow up. I craved their praise and support.

When Mother and Daddy arrived, Grandpa's soul had already departed the room. Aunt Lois sat silently. I quickly told Mother what happened and what Grandpa had seen.

Still not saved myself, I later asked if Grandpa saw Jesus or Satan's messenger that afternoon. My mother, the champion of religion in our family, would assure me that he was in heaven for sure. We must have all felt better for Grandpa being in a better place now. I know I did.

Standing beside her father-in-law's body, Mother proudly announced the news to anyone who was listening. "Well, we all know he was saved. I was with your grandpa when the preacher took his hand and asked if he'd give his soul to Christ. Grandpa said yes."

She then looked at my daddy and said in a pragmatic tone, "That could have been you, and you would *not* have seen Jesus." Daddy looked devastated, issuing not even a grunt or scowl. Mother, always singularly focused until she achieved her goal, never overlooked an opportune moment to sell her goal of getting us all to heaven.

Mother's Past

A S I APPROACHED MY TEENAGE YEARS, MY MOTHER HAD an unusual way of trying to control me. She used graphic threats and so convinced me of her probable follow through on the ultimatums that I lived in terror of the possibility that I'd stray. I shivered each time she announced to anyone within earshot, "If Donna Jene gets pregnant, I'm going to put her in a girls' home." Daddy ignored Mother's pronouncements and looked at me with a smidgen of pity.

Embarrassed by her threats, I mostly tried to ignore her rants. For good measure she made sure to inform all her female friends—in my presence—about my potential excommunication from the family. I was relieved when they didn't ask questions or comment on my budding sexuality as a young woman.

My mom was suspicious of every boy I knew, except my brothers. She always seemed to dislike males in general and was quick to criticize most men for any little transgression they might do.

I made sure I never went too far sexually with any of my dates. I knew she was serious about my ending up in some facility God knows where.

My hormones raged as I anxiously awaited a date one early spring Saturday night. My new beau, two years older than me, took me to the movies and then drove around the little town of Nocona, Texas, about fifteen miles from my house. Turning onto the country road near my house, he stopped his cherry red 1957 Chevy and parked on the side of the road. Kissing me, he pulled me to him and started ramming one of his hands down my blouse.

At first I was excited, then terrified as he started edging his other hand up my leg. With every other boy I dated, a gentle push from me had stopped him. Not this one. He continued his advancement against my dissent. I began to struggle, trying to get out from under him as he unzipped his pants. Pushing his penis toward me, he began to rip my underwear. Desperate, I tried to roll out from under him and scoot away. He grew stronger and more forceful, but finally my screaming and hysterical crying stopped him.

He acted disgusted and angry as he hurriedly drove me home, neither of us uttering a word. I jumped out of his car and flew to the front door. As always, Mom was waiting up for me in the living room. In a pointed voice she asked how the night had gone, and I quickly answered in one word: "Okay." I went to my bedroom, praying she wouldn't probe more. As I lay in bed that night, my heart still racing, I wondered if he would tell his friends how he almost took my virginity. With that thought, I instantly hated him.

My mother could always smell trouble and grew suspicious of my activity from the night before.

As usual on Sunday mornings, I awoke and went to the kitchen to eat early. Daddy was not yet up, but Mother was. Without wishing me good morning, she simply peered at me and asked again, "How was last night?"—walking the night back with her question as if I had just come in from my date. This time I couldn't control my emotions. Tears welling up in my eyes, I told her how the boy had tried to force himself on me.

She was instantly irate with the boy, with me, and it seemed with everything else in her life. "I told you that boys are dangerous and will take advantage of you," she snapped as tears slowly made tracks on my cheeks.

I heard my dad stirring from their bedroom. "After Daddy finishes breakfast, I want to talk to you in your bedroom," she whispered, drawing our conversation to a close. Anticipating my mother's demeanor at that fateful meeting, I went to my room. I feared her temper, as she was unpredictable when her anger raged and would lash out at me if I misspoke.

As promised she came in later and sat beside me on my bed—a good early sign that I might escape her hand. She looked worn and thoughtful. "Donna Jene, I need to tell you a story. You're old enough to understand." She began describing her high school years near Fort Worth, long before my dad was in her life. Mother liked school and received lots of attention from her thirty-something male schoolteacher. She was flattered, having grown up in a house full of kids with little praise to go around. After months of bonding with her teacher, he offered to drive her home from school one day, as the rain was pouring and she had a two-mile walk before her. She happily agreed.

The teacher turned up a small country path before reaching the road to Mother's house. He pulled to the side of the road and began kissing her and groping her thighs. She pushed his hand back and he just laughed, pulling her toward him. Her screams went unnoticed in the woods as he pushed her dress around her thighs and thrust inside her. She lost her virginity on a lonely wet afternoon by a man who controlled her future.

It's no secret that victims of rape are more likely to have future family issues. When I was a college student studying psychology, I learned they also have higher stress levels throughout their life. They often become control addicts and lack the ability to trust others. They never fully recover from the trauma of rape. That was my mother.

Mother's life was worse than some, as she got pregnant with my older sister that day at sixteen years of age. Approaching the teacher with her predicament, he laughed at her, telling her that no one would believe her. She believed he was right and tried to conceal her pregnancy until her belly outed her circumstances. When Mother told Grandma Mattie, she was furious and slapped her daughter's face. According to Mother, her mother was never loving toward her and almost seemed resentful of her in later years. My sister, Billie, was born a few months later. Mom went back to high school, shunned and humiliated. Boys taunted her and insulted her morals. She quit school and went to work in the fields and did odd jobs for neighbors, while Mattie kept the baby.

Never one for sharing secrets or counseling sessions before that day when she sat in my room and confided in me, I realized how long Mother must have suffered mostly in silence. Armed with this information about her past, I became more aware of how much my mother had gone through and the injustice she had quietly endured. Still, she imposed her fears on me and over-protected me my entire life, using threats as a way of controlling me. Mom was tough and not easily intimidated. Her children knew her bravado was a shell, because she was also a supportive and fun mother—if she could control the situation. We knew not to challenge her.

When they met and married, Daddy essentially rescued my mother and her child from a miserable existence. Having a child out of wedlock in rural 1930s Texas was shameful, whether forced by rape or willful consent. Daddy had always been expected to marry someone worthy of his standing, and my mother did not qualify. My dad's mother came from a long Texas heritage and was proud of her Hamilton roots in America. The Hamiltons came from England, and Grandma's family could trace their lineage back many generations. Grandma Lennie was highly ambitious like her mother and wanted all her children to marry other well-to-do Texas families.

My three aunts were natural beauties and led better lives than most in our little part of Texas. My grandfather's generous oil checks to my aunts and their husbands came regularly, and the girls were not shy about allowing their father to foot their bills. My aunts spoiled me constantly, bringing pink furry sweaters and jewelry pieces from their travels. Unfortunately their kindness did not extend to my mother, especially in the beginning of my parent's marriage.

My grandmother was horrified that my daddy would marry someone with an illegitimate child, and my aunts treated Mom like the hired help. After family meals, they retired to card games and Mother was expected to help Frances the cook with piles of dishes. Mom was vocal in her resentment and often would issue defensive remarks in front of my dad's relatives. She felt they were hateful and spoiled because of Grandpa's money. It was true to some extent, but the hatefulness was mostly aimed toward my mother.

Mother complained to Daddy about her treatment, but he was silent. Daddy would never buck his mother or sisters. I never knew if he was afraid of their wrath or losing their love, but I do know he was afraid of losing his inheritance. So he sat silently, which infuriated my mother. She grew increasingly resentful of the clan, and expressed her unhappiness in front of me and the boys. Mother described her status as "the family slave girl." When she ranted to me, it made me feel guilty. "Donna Jene," she'd say, "you're lucky you look like that side of the family. They all like that." My brother Lee was born blonde and had the looks of a German bloodline. Wayne was dark-haired and more brooding. My grandparents paid for Lee's college, not Wayne's, and they always gave Lee more attention. But none of their affection for the boys compared to the love I received. I was the epitome of their ideals—blonde, outgoing, and successful in school.

They mostly ignored my sister, Billie, but she and my mother were very close. Billie had Mother's tiny frame and beautiful face, along with a delightful sense of humor. She was great fun to be around but always seemed a little distant to her half-siblings. Billie married before I could remember her being at home. She would come see us occasionally, and she and Mother would go in my parent's bedroom and whisper. I was not allowed to come in during these clandestine meetings. Billie had a penchant for bad companions. Questionable bloodlines and misfits often accompanied her. Mother was so disappointed in her husbands and lovers, but Billie was a maverick and so unlike the rest of us. I decided as I grew older that she was that way because she felt distanced from my dad's family and always wore the stepchild collar.

My brothers and I enjoyed a special closeness. Although we loved my sister, we worried about how her next sojourn would end. She would often pile her three children in a car and head out for months without a trace. Mother was in a constant state of stress during these times when Billie went underground, and she sometimes took it out on us. She'd be short and angry until she got a phone call from Billie informing her of her whereabouts. Throughout the ordeal, Daddy would keep silent. If Billie needed money, Mother would needle Daddy and make him feel guilty until he agreed. Beaten down, he never complained. My parents paid for her to move eleven times in one year. She was always a rolling stone until her later years.

Mother blamed her own dysfunction on the way Daddy's family treated her. They had ignored and resented her from the time she was a young wife—never giving her a chance. As for me, I remain mostly confused about who was to blame for how things turned out.

Circumstances change slowly in families. My mother held on to her resentment to her grave. Daddy was the last member of his family to die when Mother was 86. After Daddy's funeral, we rode home together. With a tiny hint of satisfaction, she looked over at me and said, "Well, I outlived them all." Never one to concede failure, Mother took joy in the fact that she'd won the final match. My brothers and I weren't surprised. Her pride gave her great comfort.

Shattering Innocence

MY CORNER OF OUR HOUSE WAS THE BEST PLACE TO watch the raging West Texas windstorms and rain clouds. I could see for miles across the Texas plains from my bedroom window.

It's easy to layer over our memories of those things that frighten and jolt us awake in the middle of the night without warning. My memory of a particular windstorm is always traumatic whenever it surfaces uninvited. Although, like a well-worn coat, my recollection of what may have been the worst night of my life seems to soften with age.

Our family's front door was always open to anyone needing a meal or a welcome respite from whatever impediments the cruel environment offered. On that night the visitor was a forty-something man making his way up Highway 81 to Oklahoma. He found himself temporarily caught in high winds and hail—the best recipe for a tornado—and pulled up to our home seeking shelter.

I can still hear my dad answer the door. "Come in out of the storm," Dad offered the skinny, khaki-clad traveler. He smiled through the screen door and entered our home. Mom, who always had something left over in the refrigerator, found a slice of meatloaf and a random piece of fried chicken and served it to the stranger. He sat with my dad at our kitchen table and they made small talk. Meanwhile, black clouds continued their perilous path toward our direction.

Storms usually gave us ample warning to take cover when they got too bad because the land to our west was like a perfect pancake. No trees, no houses, just a plain vista—not particularly beautiful in any way but ideal for spotting trouble on the horizon. If we were not properly sheltered by the time the storm arrived, there was no one to blame but us. My mother was always vigilant that we not miss school. Unless dangerous winds had taken someone's life in our small community, school was in session the morning after every storm.

"The boys and you need to go to bed," Mother announced the night the stranger came inside our home. The eternal optimist, she was willing to bet that there'd be school in the morning. West Texas life would prevail against the storm's anger once more. But something else, some other danger, was brewing and carried no fair warning.

I loved lightning and had a season ticket to some great light shows from the comfort of my bed. I knew the cycles of the storm from an early age. First came the increased winds, followed by dark clouds full of dust gathered from farms along its journey, ever hungry for more dry land.

Next came raindrops spattering like chirping birds foretelling what's to come. Finally the wind gusts and blowing rain descended as the eye of the storm neared. Then the calm. All was over for another night. Covers pulled high, it was time to sleep until the next intrusion.

Sleeping peacefully as only an eight-year-old can do, I startled awake. Thinking initially that my mother was taking me from my bed to protect me from a second storm, I quickly realized that this was different. Unfamiliar hands maneuvered my pajamas, accompanied by the rhythmic sound of heavy breathing. One hand reached down the front of my bottoms, and another hand snaked up my stomach to my tiny, emerging breasts. I suddenly realized it was the traveler in my bed, roughly exploring my young body.

I didn't scream or alarm anyone and waited for a few seconds— almost enjoying a sensation foreign to my flesh. But then fear began to grip me. I didn't know what his next move was, but I was suddenly afraid of this intruder. I instinctively knew he meant harm to me and pleasure to him.

I rolled over and away, startling him. But he pursued—hands exploring and now probing. Even as a child, my fight or flight tendencies superseded my curiosity. What could I do? He was heavy now against my body. Not wanting to cause a scene, I knew only that I had to get away. I suddenly sat straight up, rolled off the opposite side of the bed, and ran to my mother's bedroom. I was a woman-child now, but my instinct to be protected was paramount.

"Mom, I'm scared of the storm. Can I sleep with you?" I remember her sleepily saying that the storm was over, but she never turned away any of us kids who were scared. I climbed in her bed and got as close to her as possible. I thought briefly of the perpetrator somewhere inside our home. I wondered if he had gone back to my brothers' room and the cot provided for his peaceful slumber.

The next morning I dressed for school and was relieved to learn that the traveler had already left our house. I watched cars from the school bus window, thinking he might be waiting for me when I got off the bus steps. Thankfully I didn't see anything that resembled his vehicle.

I could not concentrate on my studies that day and suddenly looked at my girlfriends with a different perspective. Had they already encountered a grown man shattering their innocence too? Were they hiding the insult, as I planned to do?

Just as the wind had moved on from our tiny town, so did this man. But I knew the wind always returned with a vengeance. I didn't know what a stranger might do to a little girl who was in on his secret. I've buried this memory handily in my psyche, never recalling it even when I hear of pubescent girls being raped. But it's in the most unlikely times and circumstances that I still feel his finger touching my vagina with his other hand groping my chest.

I hate that man even today for stealing my innocence and throwing it away. I'd like to inflict pain on him, but I have a gnawing feeling he is dead by now. I imagine him dying a sad and miserable ending. Cognizant that there were likely other innocent little girls in his path, I wonder where they are and if they are okay today.

We never saw the stranger again to my knowledge. No menacing winds ever delivered him to our doorstep. Maybe in his hunt for other innocent prey a benevolent tornado flipped his car, breaking his neck—a befitting death as he broke others' souls.

I told my mother many months afterward what happened. She appeared stricken, but stoic. I expected her to put her arms around me and cry. Instead she said, "Let's never talk about this again. What happened, happened. Just be careful when you're around older men."

She busied herself in the kitchen and I learned an early valuable lesson. Your pain is your pain, and no one can take away your responsibility to deal with your own mind. Shame and guilt can affect a young girl early on, especially as it relates to her body sexually.

True to Mother's advice, I was careful around older men for years. I was never alone with any man my senior, regardless of what seemed their basic good nature. Of course my grandfather symbolized everything good in a man and this incident left my feelings for him untainted. I would have loved to tell him what that man had done to his precious granddaughter, but never did. I felt a sense of responsibility after my discussion with my mother—I must forever keep this heinous secret, never divulging my part, even if it was tiny and innocent. I never wanted to upset my grandfather by telling him how my innocence had been threatened.

PART 2

Pregnant

I MARRIED A MAN I'D KNOWN MY WHOLE LIFE AND WAS
pregnant with our first child in the 1970s Nixon era. Millions of
baby boomers were graduating and we were lucky to get jobs amid
the persistent poor economy. With little prospects for gainful
employment and a belly that could barely be hidden under bulky
clothes, I turned every stone to get any job I could.

My sister-in-law's brother Homer, whom I had grown up with, was
four years older than me.

Whip smart, he had become the darling employee of the state in
the Abilene, Texas, office and I had asked my sister-in-law to get him
to recommend me. I got an interview and a chance to take the test
required in those days to be a Texas state employee. My potential
supervisor seemed to like me during the interview. I always did well

in interviews as I was chipper, cooperative, and only asked questions that made the interviewer look smart. Conceived in September 1974, my unborn was showing signs of healthy activity, kicking me hard throughout the day. Interviewing carrying a four-month old fetus was risky. Pregnancy was a disability and not discussed at work ever! I could have been found out at any time, but luckily, all stayed clandestine and I was hired. I hated the tedium of the job but loved my coworkers. One of the workers my age was also pregnant and so fun to be with that forty years later, I'm still best friends with Nancy!

Being pregnant, I felt particularly vulnerable to the gods of nature. The slick, icy streets of Wichita Falls, Texas, loomed hazardous to me and to my unborn. A college graduate, I now said both words, Wichita Falls, when referring to where I worked. Traveling to other nearby towns to fulfill demands as a social worker would inevitably lead to having flat tires, encountering cattle on the highways, and, as always, meeting the north winds bringing icy sheets of sleet that were impossible to navigate safely.

The training for my new job was to be completed in Lubbock, Texas, hours away from Wichita Falls. The state paid for the mileage, so I would drive myself back and forth between the cities weekly for one month. On weekends I'd drive back to my husband and our rented house in Wichita Falls. Five months along, evidence of my pregnancy was rapidly approaching. I just had to keep this pregnancy a secret until I got through training and a probation period. Thank God my chubby legs had since left me, as I was in tiptop physical shape after having played basketball at Midwestern University. Being tall, I carried my baby boy well without a big, poufy belly.

The second week, I headed out for training at 5:00 A.M. in iffy weather circumstances. The West Texas wind was bringing a snowstorm to all West Texas. With no idea what conditions I would meet on the road, I left extra early and wore a heavy coat, gloves, and boots in case I had to walk and leave the car on the highway. Youth does bring optimism. Now I know I'd have frozen to death, even with my accoutrements.

About an hour's drive from Lubbock, the wind was gusting harder and icy snow was blowing. My car heater was on full blast and Frankie Valli was singing one of his last hits, "My Eyes Adored You." The pick-up truck coming toward me had a horse trailer attached. I shined my lights on bright so I could be easily recognized in a silver Malibu with monthly payments of $235.

The truck braked suddenly from what I suspect had been a deer or some creature crossing the highway. The horse trailer started sliding to the right, almost disconnecting itself with its shivering inhabitants from the truck bed. I slowed to all but a standstill watching the spectacle and breathing rapidly.

The trailer eventually did disconnect and turned violently on its side. The pick-up finally stopped and a skinny farm boy jumped out of the driver's door and rushed to trailer. The horses were bellowing and snorting, obviously in distress.

I stopped on the right side of the road with my coat in hand and stupidly crossed the median. The boy was crying and trying to move the top horse off the bottom one. I was helpless watching this drama unfold.

Cell phones were non-existent, and the nearest town several miles away. Yelling through the snowy blasts, I told the boy to be careful and I would go get help. He seemed in shock, his two mares still snorting and screaming in pain. I drove faster than one would advise, getting to the tiny town of Crosbyton, Texas, in a few minutes. Two police cars parked in front of an aging coffee shop caught my eye and I pulled in. I hurried through the dirty glass door and approached the highway patrolmen, telling them of the situation. They thanked me, threw down some coins, and quickly spun one of the patrol cars east, blaring the siren and lights.

I needed my job and would be late if I followed them back to the site. So I quickly used the ladies room, got a piece of the apple pie tempting customers from underneath a glass dome, and bought a cup of coffee with milk. I pointed my car west toward Lubbock, still fighting Mother Nature all along the highway.

The wind blew, the snow swirled, and the ice pelted. Whether a woman with child, a horse with a broken leg, or a timid farm boy scared out of his wits, the weather was insistent. Life is hard in the hardscrabble environment of this lonely stretch of the USA. I hit the Lubbock city limits with snow covering my Malibu and my hands aching from gripping the wheel for about four hours. I made the training class and said nothing of what had happened. Complaining in the workforce in 1975 was not acceptable. Jobs were scarce and baby boomers looking to replace you were plentiful.

I had nightmares for years thinking of the pain those poor horses endured. I wonder if a sheriff put them to rest with his .45 pistol. The farm boy's crying has never left me and the memory revisits whenever I see a trailer behind a pick-up truck on icy roads.

Cloud Nine

CLOUD NINE IS NOT HIGH ENOUGH TO DESCRIBE how I felt when I interviewed with the pharmaceutical giant Burroughs Wellcome. My state job was fine, but I wanted more. Fate stepped in when one of my college professors called me one evening after I'd worked at my state office all day.

"Burroughs Wellcome is a great company," he told me. "They're interviewing candidates on campus next week. I know you're working, but I thought you might like to talk to them."

I had no idea what the job was or if I'd want it. Without a business degree, I assumed I might be directed to Human Resources. But I loved new challenges. The following week I had what I thought was a pleasant interview with a company representative until he simply concluded our time with the words, "I'll call you back, if we are interested." Yikes! My anxiety level prepared me to hear silence thereafter.

The call came the next Tuesday and surprised me. They wanted to interview me again Thursday at 10:00 A.M. in Plano, Texas. Wichita Falls was about three hours away. I decided to start driving at 6:00 Thursday morning, giving me an extra hour to account for the possibility of making wrong turns in my trek to Plano. GPS had not yet been invented, so I plotted my course by map. When I drove home from work Wednesday evening, the January wind blew frigid. I didn't worry, as I hoped the sun would warm everything up the next day. As I was changing clothes, I heard the TV weatherman excitedly announce, "A Blue Norther is blowing in late tonight." North Texans and southern Oklahomans are said to have coined this term. It's the most miserable circumstances imaginable. Dangerous winds gust from the north, blowing ice, rain, sleet, and snow with a vengeance. Baby calves often freeze beside their mothers, and the farmland is covered with muddy ice. Roads become impossible to navigate. The wind piles the snow into large banks and ice blankets every inch of pavement. Many times schools close, as the buses cannot maneuver the mayhem this kind of storm creates.

My husband was against my working in business, and especially a company from England like Burroughs Wellcome. Our marriage was troubled, and I suspected he had noticed the dog-eared book, *Fear of Flying*, on my nightstand. Insecure and afraid, with a two-year-old I adored, my baby boy and I stayed in a loveless situation, much like the heroine in that iconic novel. I felt edgy and nervous as I made dinner that night, thinking the wind was on my husband's side, trying to scuttle my interview. My chance of going to Plano early on Thursday was nearing zero, as more roads became impassable by the minute.

"Call the man and cancel your interview," my husband demanded. I hesitated to do so. Something said, "This is your chance, take it!" The only call I made that night was to my mother. "Would you keep Brandon tomorrow?" I whispered. "I'm going to Plano." My grandchild's overprotective angel responded, "Have you lost your mind? You can't get to my house, much less Plano, in this weather."

By now I was determined. If the highway patrol would let me, I planned to drive my Malibu south to the Dallas suburb of Plano, come what may. I laid out my best business suit and packed the car with a heavy coat, gloves, and some food and water in case I slipped off the road. I packed Brandon's warmest snugglies and took two heavy quilts to wrap us in if we had to walk in snow banks and ice. I was leaving for Plano at 4:00 A.M.

The alarm went off at 3:00 A.M. I dressed quietly, not disturbing my husband. The Norther was unrelenting. I was frightened to open the front door and meet the blast of wind, my enemy, full face as it attempted to rob me of my future. In the darkness I could see by streetlight how the ice covered every inch of our street. I would have to drive on solid ice for hours. Still, it was worth the chance. I felt driven in my heart to secure a better life for myself and my son.

My parents had reluctantly agreed to meet me on the road to Dallas, as they would encounter similarly perilous conditions, yet they would never have let one of their children down. Without cellphones to communicate, they waited on a highway in Bowie, Texas. I was almost an hour later than expected when I saw Dad's pick-up. I brushed back my tears. The wind may have been against me, but Mother and Dad were firmly on my side.

I handed off the baby, kissed his cheek, and hugged my mom. Daddy was concerned; Mother was frantic. "Are you sure?" they questioned me.

"I'll make it," I resolved. "I'll call you from Plano."

The wind howled, blowing snow across the road and blinding my sight. No other drivers matched my stupidity, having stayed home. The long stretch of ice looming ahead of me was mine to navigate. I drove south, thinking the Norther surely couldn't reach Dallas.

My hands gripped the wheel, my jaw clenched, and my head throbbed. My pain was made sharper from my spouse's not so subtle hopes that I'd fail. I silently prayed, "I can't lose this chance. I'll get to Plano." The road signs before each little town promised I was getting closer to freedom. I didn't know what the future would look like, but I knew that if I got the job I could manage the future whatever it brought.

My neck muscles throbbing, at last I saw a sign that Dallas was only forty miles away. I'd driven slowly most of the way, hoping I'd allotted enough time. Now as I approached my destination, I worried I'd be late. Losing an interview because of tardiness was not an option, Mother Nature be damned. The roads were clearing, the Blue Norther weakening to the south. I sped up a little, never considering the Burroughs Wellcome manager might have canceled the interview schedule since Plano had bad weather too.

I followed my map and saw a sign for the Plano city limits. Now I just had to make it to the I-75 IHOP restaurant where we planned to meet. Never stopping for relief along my journey, I entered the restaurant bound for the ladies room. Optimism, determination, and youth were on my side. I came out of the bathroom looking for a man I didn't know, but fortunately there were not that many people in the restaurant.

A man stood up in an overcoat and moved toward me. He was smiling and shaking his head. "You must be Donna," he said, extending his hand. I smiled. "You're the only interview candidate I couldn't get by phone last night. So I thought I'd better show up just in case you came. All my other interviews canceled."

I studied his eyes and smile. I liked this man. "But," I silently concluded, "he must think I'm desperate, which is not good." We bonded over hot coffee. He asked me a few questions, including why I'd fought the elements to have this interview. I secretly wanted to say, "You're my escape route into a new life." But instead I smiled and said I was determined to get this job.

He later told me I was his only interview. He never got back to any of the rest of the candidates. A woman driving alone for six hours in the worst weather was Burroughs Wellcome material.

Gene was a fabulous boss and great mentor for me. I loved that company and loved him as only a grateful employee could. My ticket to the future. Thank you, England!

Sometimes the harshest wind is still helpful, transporting rain to the West dry lands. This time it helped me demonstrate my mettle. Mother Nature put up a mighty roadblock, and overcoming it made me all the more determined to define my own future.

Sex for Grades

A S A STUDENT I WAS IMPRESSED THAT SEVERAL
teachers in my tiny high school had master's degrees. My
English teacher was my idol. She took particular interest in me, often
encouraging me to write poetry, which I still do today. I was fascinated
that she had a master's degree in literature. My cousin Tommy had
a master's degree in something. I didn't know how to get one for
myself, but I was determined that I would do so someday.

When I was working full time and raising my first child, those
priorities consumed my time and energy. But the promise I'd made
to myself never left me. I had to get my master's. Every semester that
I was not enrolled in graduate school seemed a waste to me. Finally I
enrolled in night classes and thus marked the beginning of my next
journey.

Mom filled in as surrogate mother to my son while I was in school. Earning 36 semester hours to get my advanced counseling degree felt like eternity. Night after night I sat in class with exhaustion as my constant companion. As my training continued it was increasingly more difficult to schedule the courses I needed in a timely and sequential manner. Finally, when I was down to one last class and a thesis to write, I could see the light. I was close but still far away.

The professor in that one remaining class was vitally important to achieving my goal. He was the conduit to the graduate committee, a shadowy, faceless group that would determine my fate. He was overly friendly and had eyed me night after night, aware of my stress. Offering to tutor me independently, I was flattered but just didn't have time for studying outside of class.

I needed to submit my thesis to the committee by mid-May in time for a summer graduation. But between a toddler needing time and attention and a job that consumed my daytime hours, when could I write? By late April I had not scribbled a word and could not concentrate at home. So I made an alternate plan. I booked an inexpensive motel room near where I lived. I would check in on Friday, hoping to check out late Sunday afternoon with a completed thesis. My mom packed an ice chest of Cokes and food for two days and nights. I told myself I would not check out of the motel until I had a thesis in hand, regardless of its quality.

I spent 36 hours reading and writing, investing the other twelve hours in fitful sleep. By 6:00 on Sunday evening, I had a rough outline for my thesis that I would submit to the committee. I had no confidence it would be accepted.

On Monday morning I was anxious about calling my professor

who now served as my official thesis adviser, as I was fully aware that I was dependent on this man to get an audience with the graduate committee. He held my future in his hands and he knew it. My professor became my unwelcome pursuer. He asked me to meet him at a bar sometime during the week so we could have a drink and celebrate my progress. Instantly I knew that without meeting him at the bar, my thesis would never reach the committee. I felt trapped and exhausted, but determined.

I said, "I'll meet you on Wednesday," relenting to his request. We met, drank wine, and laughed, although I was a fit of nerves. He smiled and seemed to believe that I actually found him attractive. When I asked him if he'd read my thesis, seeking feedback, he did not answer. When we finished the bottle of Chianti, he asked me to go to his apartment.

Country people have an adage for reluctantly agreeing to do something you feel you must do. You are said to "smile through your teeth." I smiled just this way and mechanically nodded "yes."

As I drove to his apartment, I was desperate to think of how I could keep this powerful seducer at bay and yet have time to convince him to champion my thesis. I'd blame my monthly period as the reason why I could not have sex with him. His apartment was loaded with books and candles, but what stood out prominently were the blankets on the floor and a wine bottle with glasses nearby. The windows were open, allowing a cool breeze in the room. I was obviously one of many students to perform in his woolen lair. His sex life must have been extra active during graduation season.

Once in his apartment, he began to paw at me. I wouldn't let this happen, but I did allow him to kiss me as I whispered my dilemma in his ear. He was disappointed, even almost angry. I was a bundle of nerves yet trying to be friendly. I needed this man's help to get my coveted degree. I knew I was a borderline fraud, but I had no remorse. I so wanted to tell the president of the university about this sexual coercion afterward, but I knew I'd be discounted and maybe never graduate. So I played the age-old game that many women have played.

He was irritated but told me that the graduation thesis committee was to meet the following week. Again, I asked him if he'd recommend me. Gloating with power, he agreed to approve my thesis. I left soon after, promising a future rendezvous. I made sure the date was after the committee met, silently praying that I'd never have to see him again. Several days later, a representative of the committee notified me that I was approved to graduate at the end of the second summer session.

My answering machine blocked several of his calls after that, his voice growing more aggressive each attempted contact. I never returned his calls and never revisited the psychology classroom. I told few people what had transpired, as I knew my motives would be questioned as well as my behavior. The late Seventies offered little protection for women being sexually abused in the professional world.

Walking in the graduate processional, I was acutely aware that he was seated in the section reserved for faculty. As the president handed me the sheepskin I so wanted, I felt his eyes boring into my back. I wondered how many students had succumbed to his influence.

I still get a stomach knot whenever I recall his beard and heavy breathing. I received no joy from stringing him along, but I would do the same thing again if necessary. Women have survived for centuries by being great actors.

A Businesswoman

B Y SUNDAY THE WIND WAS RESTING AND THE SNOW had melted. I was giddy over my new job and chipper around the house. I was a "businesswoman." The phone rang Sunday night. My new boss said I'd need to spend the month of March in Research Triangle Park, North Carolina, to complete the required training for all new reps. My mind went to the baby and spending a month away from him. Wow.

I quickly called my mother to see if a month was okay for him to stay with her and Dad. "Of course," she said. I was relieved and overjoyed at the same time. Our one orange wall phone was in the kitchen adjacent to the den. My husband was agitated, as he'd heard me talking on the phone to my new boss.

"Call him back and tell him you're not taking the job," he half-yelled from the den. My heart broke at his words. I wanted the job. I wanted my marriage and to be a good mother. But his tone was resolute. I floundered briefly. What should I do?

Somewhere inside my torn psyche, I gathered courage. "I will not," I responded, unmoved. "I am taking the job."

He stormed out the door. I cried. The future was in front of me, but my legs were weak. Could I move forward?

I waited for my employment paperwork to arrive by mail. My plan was to sign it, give two weeks' notice of termination to the State of Texas, and find my own place to live when I returned from North Carolina. Hesitant to discuss my marital issues with my parents, I felt panicked. I wanted to rent a safe apartment in a good part of Wichita Falls, the city that would remain my hub for detailing legal drugs to doctors around the North Texas area. I could find reliable day care for the baby, and if I overnighted for work, my mother would gladly be my Mother Teresa to help her grandson.

I called my parents. "I'd like to talk to you," I said. They lived about twenty miles away, so I packed the baby in his carrier for our afternoon meeting. I made sure I would be home to prepare dinner. They were waiting for me. Mother got the baby settled and we all sat at the kitchen table. I told them my plan to move to an apartment. "I plan to get a divorce," I announced. I expected to meet with shame and cautious warnings not to do so. Instead my father broke his vow of rarely speaking in stressful situations and said, "We wondered why you stayed so long." It was over.

The paperwork came, and I signed and planned my resignation. My coworkers seemed surprised that I would leave a stable job for the unknown, while my friend Nancy championed my freedom. She knew my home life.

I said nothing of my apartment lease to my husband. I wanted my things left in place while I was gone. I was excited but frightened. He threatened to take the baby if I left. But I knew he'd have to get through my family first. West Texas winds were tougher than him, and I was from a family of survivors.

The wind flew me to North Carolina. I loved putting on a professional business suit in my hotel room. My mom had bought me three suits in Wichita Falls, and my dad paid for my deposit and first month's rent on my apartment. They were cohorts to my escape, and our love for each other helped us execute the plan.

I never considered failure, but some of the trainees were sent home. I was a stranger among newly graduated Ivy Leaguers. Most top-tier companies wanted well-known schools on employees' résumés. My state school was unknown to most of my classmates, but they quickly respected my studious nature and willingness to learn.

Three weeks into my month-long training sessions, I had a blinking message waiting for me on my hotel room phone. Thinking it was my husband calling to issue another threat, I dreaded the message. I called the front desk to retrieve my message and was initially relieved to learn that it was my mother. But then I realized that something could have happened to the baby. I called her immediately.

"Mother, I see you called me," I said, getting ready to go out as I talked to her. I had planned to meet my classmates for dinner. We had expense accounts, although not princely ones.

"I wanted you to know that we're okay," she informed me in an excited voice. I stopped changing clothes and focused on the conversation on the other end of the line. "Oh my God," I thought. "Did my husband try to take the baby?"

Mother calmly continued, "Daddy lost the barn, but we were in the cellar. Brandon is okay. We saw the tornado from the storm shelter's window." She described how the twister blew right through the southwest part of the yard and made a direct hit on the barn. What a sight. "But thank God we are okay," she added. My heart stopped racing just long enough to respond to this awful tragedy that had come so close to hurting my family. "Tell Daddy I'm sorry about the barn," I told her. "Mom, I love you all. I'll see you in a week." I hung up the phone.

To my surprise my husband was at the airport when I arrived home the next week after completing my training. He and the baby were at baggage claim waiting for me. Instead of being happy, I was suspicious and terrified that he would use Brandon as leverage for me to quit my job. I tried to remain calm as various bags circled in front of me until my luggage came into view. He grabbed my bag when it appeared, and I took the baby as we walked to the Malibu parked outside. I was stunned when I saw my mother and dad in the car.

Mother told me later that she didn't want my husband to take the baby without her and Dad being present. So they asked if they could come with him to pick me up that day. Their strength and resolve still amaze me decades after.

On the hours-long drive home, everyone was mostly silent. I wished so much that I could tell them about my adventures as a newly minted businesswoman, but I knew my stories would irritate the situation and make it worse than it was.

That weekend I delivered the news. "The baby and I are moving to an apartment," I told him. He could keep the house, I said. I only needed a few days to move. My parents and two brothers would help me. Tempers flared at my revelation, and I drove to my parents' house, not knowing if my possessions back at the house would remain safe. I hurriedly took my business suits and baby clothes, and as I did so, I felt my future was set. Nothing could stop me now.

* * *

MY FIRST MONDAY ON the job, I had appointments all week. On Tuesday and Wednesday I would be in Altus, Oklahoma, meeting with doctors. I knew nothing of the wind's upcoming devious plans to thwart my future.

I met with doctors in Altus on Tuesday as planned and intended to spend a restful night in a local motel. Tomorrow night, I'd thought I'd go to my mother's and see my little one.

I settled in and turned on the television. Three channels was the sum total of all television available in 1979. I tried both of the two Wichita Falls channels and got no reception, settling instead for a Lawton, Oklahoma, broadcast. I noticed the weatherman frantically pointing to a map of the entire North Texas-Southern Oklahoma region. He began screaming a dire warning to the television audience, "Take shelter now!"

I was stunned and scared at the same time. The storm had descended on Wichita Falls, Lawton, and all the nearby farms and ranches. Several tornadoes had been spotted, and television cameramen were busy tracking each location. The clouds were angry as they sent out their henchmen. I envisioned my parents and son. Were they in the path of destruction?

Terrified, I dialed my mother's number. No answer. I called the desk clerk. "Do you know what's happening in Wichita Falls and the area?" I asked. She was nonplussed, adding only that Altus, my location, was the only city *not* being hit by twisters. My relief lasted only a second when I realized my family could be blown away. I called again. No one answered.

I grabbed my purse and went to the front desk to tell the clerk I was leaving for Wichita Falls. She said matter-of-factly, "You can't drive on the roads. They are closed down!"

The deadly wind had won the battle, but I told myself I'd get to my family somehow. I waited all night, glued to the one station that was reporting for news about the outcome. I learned that one that more than one tornado had hit Wichita Falls and Lawton, with Wichita Falls receiving the worst of it. People were injured and dead. No one was sure how many.

Dawn brought an eerie calm with little wind. The weary television reporter said that only residents of Wichita Falls could enter the city limits, such was the devastation. I called my mom's phone number one more time. She answered.

"Mom! Are you and the baby alright?" I practically screamed into the phone.

"Yes," she said, sounding exhausted. "We stayed in the cellar all night." This storm was far worse that the one that had taken the barn a few days ago. "This storm was the worst I've ever seen," she confessed. She told me how the television had reported that Altus, Oklahoma, was safe. All night she had hoped that I had made it to Altus and was not out on the road somewhere. I assured her I had spent a sleepless night in the motel worrying about them.

Before dawn I left for Wichita Falls to see the damage. I tried to drive to my new apartment. Fortuitously, my parents had moved only a few of my clothes and some belongings the week before. A tired-looking patrolman stopped me. "Miss, you can only enter this street by foot. Do you live there?" I couldn't answer directly. I began to explain that I was leaving my husband and had partly moved in. Did that count? He had no time for counseling me. People were dying.

He let me go, and I parked and began walking through rubble to my intended apartment. The scene unfolding before me was like that of a war zone. When I got to what was left of my apartment, all I could see was a telephone table with a beige phone on top of it. Almost as if the dead could call heaven directly and ask for aid. I cursed the clouds as the sun started to shine.

The town of Wichita Falls was in shock. Thirty-plus dead and many hurt. Hospitals were overflowing, and the national news stations were flying small planes to this West Texas hellhole. The 1979 Wichita Falls tornado is still reported as one of the deadliest in history.

When I arrived at my mother's house later, I hesitantly called my new boss, knowing I should be working that day. Telling him of my plight with nowhere to live, he gave me instant hope. "Come to the Metroplex," he said." I have a temporary opening between Fort Worth and Dallas called the Mid-Cities and you're bound to find some decent housing nearby." It sounded like heaven compared to the nightmare I'd just seen.

I didn't know where I was going to live. But one thing was for certain. I would not leave my baby boy for a tornado to devour. He would go with me wherever I went from then on.

West on Highway 183

DRIVING WITH MY TODDLER IN MY COMPANY CAR, I left my mom's house, telling her I'd call her when I reached Arlington. I'd been to Six Flags over Texas several times, so I knew where the city of Arlington was. The other area called the "Mid-Cities" was a total mystery, so I planned to make our new home in Arlington instead.

We drove down small two-lane roads that are now super highways. At what seemed like a major intersection, I stopped for gas. As I paid, the attendant asked me where I was going. Was it that obvious that I was confused and lonely?

I found myself suddenly spilling my emotions to this total stranger. I was leaving my husband, taking my baby, and trying to find a place to live today, I told him. All I owned was in my car. The tornado had destroyed or my husband had possession of the rest. The stranger advised that I should go west on Highway 183 and I'd hit Bedford, Texas, in just a few minutes. It had nice apartments, he said with a soft smile. Knowing nothing to the contrary, I took his advice and headed west.

Brandon and I soon entered the offices of the Soto Grande apartment complex in Bedford. Armed with a check for a deposit and a few clothes in the trunk, the apartment manager showed us a downstairs apartment. Done—two bedrooms, two baths!

The apartment was very humid and hot, but it was located on a nine-hole golf course and had a nice pool. The electricity was off, as it turned out, and it was too late in the day to make a deposit at the local utilities office.

To escape the heat I opened all the windows and the sliding glass door. I made a pallet and slept on the floor with my baby on my first night as a single mother, willing the slightest breeze to make its way into our muggy apartment. The next morning, my new and curious neighbor told me there'd been a rape last night and wanted to make sure my doors were locked. Perhaps fate kept the rapists from my open door. Maybe God thought I'd already had enough stress.

I needed to get back to work and looked for day care centers for the baby. I took him to the first one I came across and registered him there. Fighting tears, I made it only a few miles away but could still see him crying for his mommy. I turned around, went back to the day care center and put him in my car, and drove to Mother's house eighty miles away, wondering if she would keep him until I got settled in the city.

"Of course," Mother said, stretching out her arms toward him. And I cried again.

Although short on funds, I bought a few pieces of furniture and some house goods. My electricity was finally connected, and I hung my few things in the closet. Is this my future, I wondered. Little money, no friends, and my baby so far away from me?

* * *

INITIALLY MY HUSBAND THREATENED me with a custody suit for Brandon. I had to travel for work and be away from my child. I was devastated, caught between two unsatisfying options.

I still don't understand why I picked up a community paper and looked in the want ads that day. One ad stood out to me.

"I NEED A FAMILY," the ad announced. I read on and discovered a healthy grandma who would like to live with a family needing childcare, cooking, and cleaning. I instantly called the number. Disappointed that a man answered the line, I assumed I was too late.

"Oh no," he said. "It's my mother who wants to work. She moved in with my family a few months ago, but there's not much for her to do," he explained. "She has to stay busy," he added with a chuckle.

Ma Helen was a godsend. She understood my plight as only a mother could. For $100 per month and her food, she would care for Brandon, cook, and clean. She could not drive, but we lived very close to the grocery store. She loved to bundle up the baby in his stroller and take off on an adventure. I'll never lose the memory of Ma Helen pushing the baby down the sidewalk in his stroller, both happy as could be.

We became a sweet family. Ma Helen was my city mother and

Brandon's city grandmother and we grew to love each other. When I changed jobs and worked for my dream company, Procter and Gamble, I started in sales. They promoted me to management in less than a year. As my money situation improved with every promotion, so did my feeling of self-worth because I could finally provide for my family and be independent.

A single parent with total responsibility for every part of my child's life, I took motherhood seriously and tried to work around all of Brandon's preschool events. It was a relief to know that if I got stuck on the road, whether from a delayed flight or traffic jam, Ma Helen would be there for all of us. She was my rock.

My management position with P&G demanded that I work monthly with my salespeople who were scattered throughout Texas. I still have a vivid memory of sitting on the airport runway in Houston trying to get home for a nursery school play. My guilt was overwhelming, as I imagined the other mothers clapping while my chair beside Ma Helen was empty.

When the pilot announced that high winds between Dallas and Houston were grounding the plane for a few hours, I cursed my old enemy, the wind. Just when I felt as if I had regained control over my life, the wind would remind me that my fate had never left its hands.

The day would come five years later when I would tell Ma Helen that I was marrying a nice man named Bruce that I worked with at Procter and Gamble. She said she was pleased, and neither of us addressed what this meant. The next day, she told me her sister needed help in Florida. "I'll just be in the way of your new family," she told me. We both cried, and she moved to Florida the next week. God had sent Brandon and me an angel to take care of us until we were safe again.

Pot, Cocaine, and Whatever

MY ATTEMPT TO MAKE HOMEMADE MARIJUANA BY drying banana leaves in my aunt's basement was a dismal failure. However, the Sixties and Seventies continued to serve as a significant influence on me and my baby boomer friends as we grew into adulthood. Drugs were plentiful at the time, and cool young people felt little danger in trying the drug du jour.

Several factors heavily influenced my decision about whether to try drugs. As a teen, just knowing that my mother would have sent me away in the same way she had threatened me about getting pregnant was enough to avoid drugs. There was no way to know for certain if she would follow through, but something told me that Mother was just crazy enough to do so.

If that wasn't enough, watching my aunt's hopeless addiction to alcohol also scared me into adulthood. Frightened I'd become addicted to drugs even with one or two trial experiences made me think twice before grabbing a joint or snorting a line of cocaine. I've always felt that I had a strong potential for addictions.

Third, by the time I had enough money or freedom to acquire drugs, I was a mother. The thought of being out of control and unable to care for my son terrified me. But more important, my ex-husband had threatened to sue for custody if I ever "misbehaved." The potential of losing my son was a complete non-starter. I would remain drug free.

While dating as a single mother, my choices were important as they related to my son Brandon. A small boy primarily spending time with only his mother, I wanted him to be around upstanding men and good male role models. I was acutely aware of this priority and made sure that no man spent the night in my home when Brandon was there.

Girlfriends were a big part of my social world, and I always loved being with other young mothers. Four of us decided to party one Saturday night in December 1979. Mother had kept Brandon for the weekend and freed me to kick up my heels.

We had perfected the youthful looks and bodies that go along with being in your late twenties. As we entered the Dallas Anatole Hotel bar with the collective confidence of a group of women out on the town, I must say that we knew we were hot! Challenging each other to find good-looking guys, I was first to make a bet—they had to give me $20 if the first good-looking man I approached asked me to have a drink with him. If he didn't, I had to throw my money in a pool for my girlfriends to scoop up.

I quickly surveyed the merchandise and fixated on a handsome, well-dressed, and dark-haired man seated at the bar. "Wow," I thought. I wasn't sure I could pull this off. He was a ten and for all my bravado with my girlfriends, I didn't know my score.

Taking a big breath, I walked to the bar and positioned myself close to this Adonis, yet still out of reach. Soon there was an open seat next to him. He and I had already caught each other's eyes, so I sexily sidled up to him. He smiled before he looked at me quizzically and asked, "What's a good Jewish boy like me doing talking to Gentile girl like you?"

I was totally perplexed, but smiled broadly.

He smiled again and I knew I'd already won the bet.

His name was Hal, I learned, as we shared a drink together. Hal was Jewish. Having grown up a Christian in the South, I had never known a Jew. I was not necessarily Baptist but always considered myself an occasional Sunday attender in a Christian church, usually seated next to my mother. I hesitated to refer to him as Jewish in our conversation. I thought he might take exception to the label. I had a lot to learn.

Before I knew it, I was on my way to developing a relationship with this handsome Northerner, a New York City Jew. I was instantly smitten. He was unlike any man I'd ever met. Unfortunately he was in Dallas on business, only coming to Texas a few times a year.

Hal came to Dallas several times the next few months. Then we both agreed that I'd visit him in New York. On my first ever trip to New York City, Hal sent a limo and driver to JFK airport to pick me up. Although I was genuinely impressed with this overture, I was also quietly disappointed that he didn't personally appear at the gate to greet me. I felt so very mature and worldly riding in the back of that limousine on my way to Long Island for the weekend with Hal.

Hal was the only son of a very successful "rag merchant," as he described his father. His dad had a national line of women's clothing and sold to major department stores. The family had a weekend place on Long Island, and Hal had invited some buddies and their girlfriends to join us there.

He answered the door when I arrived and welcomed me into the home. The house was a contemporary 1970s design with a conversation pit in the middle of the living area. Booze was plentiful and in New York style, the atmosphere was filled with loud talking among hard-charging people partying hard. Cigarette smoke swirled above everyone's heads, making me feel slightly nauseous.

The pool table was a popular spot among the guests, and I loved to play pool. Hal and I were partners in one round, but we didn't win a game against more skilled New Yorkers. Missing easy shots, Hal seemed edgy and nervous. "Let's go see the master," he invited with a coy smile. I hung up my pool stick and followed him.

To my surprise, the master bedroom was crowded with several couples lying on the floor and on top of the bed. A small table was set up by the windows, two chairs placed at each side. I saw a long-haired man bend over the tabletop for a moment then walk away.

Hal pulled out a chair at the vacant table saying, "Have a seat, my princess." Despite the chaos in the dimly lit room, I was infatuated with this Northern charmer who put me at ease. He sat in the other chair. Carefully laid out on the top of the table were lines of white powder on small sheets of paper. Without fanfare, Hal leaned over and snorted an entire line in one nostril. I was startled.

Naïve, part of me wondered if this was really cocaine, and the other half of me knew with certainty that it was. He smiled and urged me to do a line. My mind went to my son. I couldn't do this. This was dangerous. What if the police arrived? I could be arrested and lose my son forever. I could overdose and die. I firmly said no to Hal's offer.

He was woozy and swaying in the chair, but he was lucid enough to know that I had refused to join his personal party.

"Come on and try it," he insisted.

I shook my head no.

Clearly agitated, he began talking louder. "Donna, you're no fun. What's wrong with you?

You're here with my friends and embarrassing me. Just do it!" He pointed to the powder.

I refused again. "You go ahead," I said weakly. "I'm okay."

"No you're not. You're not okay!" He was practically yelling now, and I knew he was high. The other occupants of the master bedroom were beginning to notice us.

This was not the Hal I knew from our rendezvous in Texas. Disenchanted, I pushed away from the table to go to the bathroom, trying to get some space between me and the drug-induced crowd. As I stood up, Hal reached over and grabbed me so quickly that the white powder spilled to the floor, papers scattering.

This seemed to make him angry. He grabbed my hair and demanded, "You are going to do some coke! You think you're too good to party with us." My New York City boy was nothing like what I thought. Hal was clearly a drug addict and a mean one.

He was getting rough and belligerent. I pulled away and started across the darkened room. Hal bolted after me, pushing me toward the bed—a waterbed he had mentioned several times in our conversations. I stumbled and sat down abruptly on the bed frame. Hal shoved me down, trying to kiss me. I pushed him away hard. Shocked that I was so forceful, he immediately slapped me on the face.

Thankfully, he seemed to pass out after that—or maybe he just lost interest in me. Either way, I made my escape to the kitchen. A telephone directory hung on a cord beside a wall phone. No one noticed as I thumbed through the directory and called for a taxi. I grabbed my packed suitcase and handbag, making my way out the door. I waited outside the dark house on Long Island, praying that none of Hal's friends would find me.

The cab pulled up, I got in the back seat and asked to go to the JFK airport even though there were no more flights scheduled until the next day, I felt safer there than with Hal and his friends. Placing my suitcase under my seat and using my bag as a pillow, I slept fitfully on an uncomfortable leather seat in the terminal. The next morning I boarded a plane for Texas.

That night ended my infatuation with Hal. I realized that he was too worldly for this country girl and certainly for a single mother. Landing at DFW airport, I gladly drove the eighty miles to pick up my son from Mother's and held him close when I saw him. I never heard from Hal again. I sometimes wonder what happened to him and his addiction. I was so fortunate that the love of my son and the fear of my mother kept me safe from the clutches of drugs.

Pictures

AFTER ANOTHER LONELY SATURDAY NIGHT, ON SUNDAY morning I decided to read some training materials at the pool. Always fighting the sun's rays on my fair skin, I covered my legs in my favorite gauzy cover-up. The wind and I were having a tussle, each trying to control the papers on my lap.

I was disgusted by the rowdiness of the poolside scene, thirty- and forty-somethings guzzling beer and making lewd comments to willing cronies. I chose to remain aloof and uninterested, hoping no one would approach me. I was too fragile to engage with these revelers anyway.

The wind continuing its relentless tug of war, I caught a glimpse of a tanned, good-looking man walking toward me. Wearing tennis whites and holding a racket in his hand, he walked close enough to my chaise lounge for our smiles to connect. I was struck by his confidence among the poolside degenerates. He stopped to introduce himself and I learned his name was John. After exchanging pleasantries, I surprised myself when I asked him to join me.

"I'd like to, but I need to go change. But maybe I'll be back," he said.

John kept his promise, as he would many times in the next four years. He returned to the pool, pulled a folding chair next to my seat, and we engaged in a long conversation. Having a new friend was comforting to me, especially one who listened as I poured out my story.

He smiled the protective smile I would learn to appreciate so many times in the next few months. I had no idea then how much stress this stranger wound soon endure to help his new friend.

"Well, how about joining me for pasta and a glass of wine tonight? I'm a fair cook," John offered and smiled. Out of loneliness and brewing excitement, I agreed. The dinner was casual and fun.

John became my regular date. Unlike many men who would shy away from a divorcée with a young child, he seemed to embrace my circumstances. My son Brandon was never an imposition, rather a welcome addition to our dates. John became a valued surrogate father and a tremendous mentor in his life.

I traveled extensively during my first months in the city, and John (like my mother) was happy to have Brandon stay with him. When he moved to a house with three bedrooms, he told me later that he'd intended for this home to be "for all of us." Brandon had his own bedroom at John's house and they would play together.

Ma Helen was living with us, and I felt God had sent me yet another angel to help stabilize my crazy situation. My ex-husband's anger loomed over the first year of our divorce. He would call me to talk to Brandon, and upon answering his call, he would systematically berate me for my new lifestyle—one where I'd taken Brandon to the city and was now involved with another man. "What a slut," my ex would say.

Tears came often during those first months. What had I done? Maybe he was right. I'd torn up my son's home, moved to a strange city, and destabilized our lives for what? I had my independence, but was it worth the cost to my son?

* * *

THREE WEEKENDS A MONTH, on Friday nights and Sunday afternoons, I would meet my ex halfway between Fort Worth and Bowie, Texas, to exchange our son for the weekend. In my gut I knew he was saying bad things about me to Brandon. But what was I to do? John and I were developing a solid friendship and enjoyed being together. Both our lives were busy with careers and mine doubly so with Brandon's activities. When Brandon was at his dad's home, John and I had fun dates usually in Dallas.

John was highly intelligent and curious about new things. He loved new restaurants, food, wine, and travel. We planned extensive trips, always including Brandon. John respected my role as a mother and never asked or was invited to stay over at my house. My settling into a happy routine seemed to further irritate Brandon's father. He continued threatening me regularly with intentions of suing for custody. Each threat chilled me to the bone. He intuitively knew I worried over my work schedule and was terrified of losing my son. Striking my heart where it hurt the most, I know how struggling mothers feel when their kids are at stake.

Hesitant to bring John into this web, one evening I poured out my worries to him. He listened with his usual compassion. "Don't worry," he said and reached across the checkered tablecloth to touch my hand. "If we need to, we will get married. This will strengthen your case. I don't travel much, and being married will provide a stable home for Brandon." God, I loved this man for that. But marriage was not my wish. I loved my freedom and self-sufficient life. I asked if the halfcocked but generous proposal would stand if and whenever I needed it. He smiled and nodded. Again I felt genuine love.

Meanwhile my ex-husband kept making innuendos about my whereabouts on weekends, my staying over at John's house, or weekend trips with the two of us. How could he possibly know these things unless he was stalking us? I worried that he was getting angrier and might threaten us physically.

I enjoyed going to John's house when Brandon was gone, as we had privacy. Besides, Ma Helen was at my house, and I never wanted her to feel as if she was a burden on my dating life. John grew up on a farm as well, so being the two country kids transplanted to the city, we enjoyed sitting on his patio for hours talking.

Wooden blinds covered John's windows, and he and I both loved the freedom of keeping them open even at night. With my tendency to be claustrophobic, I enjoyed looking out at the glow of the nearby street light. Besides, no one could see in a darkened home. One Saturday evening we decided John would cook as I perched on his kitchen stool near the windows, happily telling him stories. I thought I faintly heard a rustling of grass but ignored it, thinking the wind must have blown the nascent tree John had planted in the backyard.

Being with John was easy and stress free, and I decided to spend the night as I had done before. But that night was different. I slept poorly, still questioning if I was wrong and hadn't seen someone snapping my picture, yet knowing it was true. John either didn't see anything or said nothing.

The next morning, I felt ill at ease. What if my ex had been stalking us and had taken a picture for some future court appearance? When I picked up Brandon later that afternoon, I didn't address the issue with my ex. How could I say, "Did you take a picture of John and me last night?"

Months went by and I remained suspicious, hoping everything would settle down. My hope was short-lived, as my ex threatened me again. This time, he told me, he had proof that I was a slut. Without question, I knew he had stalked me, snapping proof that I was in an affair. Our divorce had been final for years by then, so what damage was an affair between two unmarried lovers?

In 1980 women were thought of as mostly homemakers. Traveling for work and having a lover might prove me unfit as a homemaker and maybe as a mother. I was always on edge about losing my son. My ex took great joy in telling me he had shown a picture of John and me together to my small son. Heartsick that my son wouldn't understand, I cried as I told John what had happened. He was furious that his home had been invaded by this angry stranger. More than that, he was upset that I had been offended by anything that my ex did.

"Let's get married," John suggested once more. "I will offer you a good home and Brandon will be fine. I love him too," he told me.

Life got better when my ex remarried and it seemed to end his hostility. Although John and I dated for four years, we rarely discussed marriage—me not ready for commitment, him not ready to hear about my lack of commitment. We remained friends even after our love story came to an end. We both eventually remarried. I never stopped loving John for his generous heart and loving soul. He was a godsend at the right time for both Brandon and me.

PART 3

Linda

MOST RURAL FAMILIES LOOK TO RELATIVES TO BE their best friends. My girlfriend Diane has been and still is my best friend from the fourth grade, but my sister-in-law Linda also became my best friend and pseudo sister. She was only a few years my senior and we had much in common.

Alongside my brother Wayne, Linda would laugh and joke at our weekly Sunday lunches, a special time always reserved for family. I loved this girl-woman and felt as if I had gained a soul mate. We typically followed lunch with family croquet games on the lawn or board games inside. Linda and Mother watched contentedly as Daddy, my brothers Lee and Wayne, and I competed against each other.

Most young men worked in the oil and gas business in North Texas during the 1970s, as did Wayne. He had a good job but had to move from time to time to small Texas oil towns like Borger, Amarillo, or Shamrock, Texas—all too far away for us to see them every Sunday as we preferred.

A few years into their marriage, Linda was hospitalized in Borger after they'd lived there a while. We assumed she would be out in no time, as she was young and strong. How sick could a 35-year-old be? But she stayed in the hospital for three weeks and was eventually diagnosed with pancreatitis.

Mom, jokingly called Nurse Ratched in our family, pronounced after her diagnosis, "Thank God it's not fatal." So I quit worrying.

Wayne never did. He was so protective of Linda, caring for her as if she were a fragile doll. I loved him for his way with her. Linda's malady was much worse than we knew. We later learned that she had acute recurrent pancreatitis, an extremely painful condition. She battled the disease for decades and never complained.

When our family gathered at my mother's for holidays and sporadic weekends, we were never sure if Linda could make it. She could have a painful attack at any time. My brother never considered leaving her, thus they had to cancel family events from time to time.

Linda seemed sicker as the years went by. A dedicated elementary school teacher, she often missed days due to the deadly disease. None of us worried, however, as Mom maintained that Linda would "be okay."

* * *

By this time I was remarried to Bruce and living in the Dallas-Fort Worth suburb of Colleyville, Texas. I enjoyed working from home, as it allowed me the time to volunteer in my community and make friends with many of the Colleyville leaders. When I assumed the role of the president of the Chamber of Commerce, several residents asked me to consider local politics. I was flattered but scared. I knew nothing about city leadership. Each passing year, as more people approached me to run for local office, I would briefly consider it, then refuse because of my insecurities. I was afraid to run because I was afraid to lose.

I told my husband one day at the beginning of 1997, "If they ask me again this year, I'm going to answer, 'Never.' Or I'm going to do it." That January some city leaders approached me again. With a deep breath, I agreed.

Old friends and alliances became strained during the 1997 city council election. As a candidate myself, I felt forced to choose between two hopefuls who ran for the other remaining seats. I chose one side, not realizing how I would be hated by the other. Looking back, my new foes must have felt betrayed, as both sides had initially backed me. I won my bid for city council without an opponent but had to face the embarrassment of my new enemies erecting signs against me at the polling places.

For a country girl who loved to be loved, I was devastated. What happened? I had not yet sat in the city council chair. How could I suddenly be hated so much?

I must admit, I did feel a certain smugness over my win. However, my confidence was soon destroyed as some citizens took me to task over their assumption that I would not know what to do in office. Knowing I could lose the next election, I tried not to follow in the footsteps of those politicians who I believed were out of touch with our citizens. I wondered if they realized that the next election could bring their callous leadership to an end.

On the other hand, my supporters seemed to like me in office and even asked me to run for mayor at the end of my first council term. I considered this idea, even as my old demon—fearing failure—returned to haunt me. I felt our current mayor was too busy in his career to run the city, so I said yes.

I knew I had some support, but I was not blind to the fact that I still had some hateful outspoken enemies. I signed up for mayor and worked every day to garner votes, knocking on doors and attending events. I was not shy about asking for votes.

The citizens awarded me the office of mayor in May 1999. I was so pleased and again a little smug. Just when I began to say to myself, "I'm good at this political game," my enemies sought to ruin my reign. They were vocal in their resentment toward me and seemed determined to destroy my mayoral tenure. Although some of my previous friends became new allies of my political foes, I did not bend to their pressure. I did what I thought was best for our community and found that I had more support than I realized. Politics and leadership can be a lonely path, and I have experienced both.

Engrossed in my weighty responsibilities, I didn't get to visit my brothers much. Instead they came to see my family, as taking time to drive the two hours north was difficult for me because I inevitably had weekend duties as the mayor.

About six months into the job, my mother called. I always dreaded Mother calling because I've always hated to talk on the phone. She could talk for far longer than I wanted, and I preferred to call her so I could control the length of our conversations.

Reluctantly, I picked up the receiver. "Linda is in the emergency room, really sick," she informed me in a hushed tone. "They say she may not make it." I was stunned.

"What is wrong?" I wanted to know. Life without Linda could not exist. "Pancreatitis," Mother said flatly. I responded, "I thought you said it was never fatal." She answered, "Well, I didn't know how serious it was."

The small-town doctor gave her only two days to live in her current state. My brother decided to get her to Baylor Hospital in Dallas. I had been a board member of a Baylor affiliate and made some calls to the hospital. They care-flighted Linda for the hundred-mile journey, and Wayne drove to meet her there. Immediately I headed to Baylor Hospital, as I hoped to be there also when the helicopter landed since time was so short.

The experienced surgeons went to work and kept her alive past her initial prognosis from the other doctor. She was in intense pain and stayed in the intensive care area for months. Occasionally they downgraded her out of intensive care only to return for several more months again. She only left the hospital once after her admission for a two-day visit to my home, only thirty minutes from the hospital.

It hurt me to see her remain lucid throughout her excruciating experiences, pain shooting through her abdomen. Still, she wanted to do something meaningful for me. Knowing how much I loved her apricot fried pies, she sat at my kitchen table in her wheelchair and instructed my brother on how to construct the ingredients and then supervised the baking. I did not care if I overdosed on sugar and downed several of those pies made from her heart. Linda returned to Baylor after that precious weekend together, never to leave the hospital again.

* * *

By March 2000, Linda had been in intensive care for three years. That same month, the west wind made an ominous visit to Dallas and to Baylor Hospital. Blowing storm clouds into the city, tornados began forming to the south. Weather forecasters warned that downtown Dallas, where my dear Linda lay in a hospital bed, could be in the eye of the storm. As I watched helplessly, nurses and orderlies scampered outside Linda's room, moving patients to safer areas.

"Get the beds away from the windows!" I heard them say to one another. I was holding Wayne's hand when the orderly unhooked Linda's IVs and other lifelines and swiftly moved her to the hallway. *What a way to die,* I thought, *because of the dastardly wind.* Wayne aggressively insisted that her life-saving tubes be reinstated. The tornados skipped downtown Dallas and instead focused their fury on Fort Worth, thirty miles to the west. Fast-thinking medical personnel and the arbitrary nature of the wind saved Linda and many patients that day.

As Linda's condition rapidly deteriorated, my tenure as mayor continued. The city was progressing nicely, but my foes were bound and determined to see my demise and publicly denounced me at every opportunity. On a drive from Colleyville to Baylor Hospital, I got a text message from a concerned supporter and good friend.

"Call me immediately," it read.

Tired and weary from worry and overwork, I dialed her number.

"What's the problem?" I'd learned to ask when answering the myriad of concerns that a city leader faces.

"Are you sitting down?" she asked. "No. I'm driving, but, again, what has happened?" I was too short with her.

She excitedly explained, "An anonymous source set up a website full of propaganda against you and sent the web address to Colleyville residents. I don't know who all has received it or exactly what it says, but I have heard that whatever is on the website makes you look dishonest and weak."

I sighed weakly and to her surprise said nothing in response. Finally, she asked, "Are you alright?"

"No, I'm not alright," I said defiantly to my friend and supporter. "I don't care what the frickin' website says, and I don't care who hates me!"

"What?" she demanded. She knew how much I loved praise and desired approval.

"I just don't care," I said again, this time even more forcefully. "I don't care about anything right now except one thing." I found myself shouting into the phone, "And that's the fact that my sister-in-law is dying."

She was dumbstruck. I was devastated.

Linda died that day.

Heart and Soul

I WAS EXCITED BUT ANXIOUS WHEN I FIRST BECAME A mother. After Brandon's 1:00 a.m. arrival, the nurse laid him in my arms and I held him close. With a tiny person to care for, I worried how it was possible that I could be responsible for this life for the next eighteen years. Eighteen years seemed forever to a 25-year-old mother. The prospect was scary, but I was totally unaware that in a few short years I would become this baby's primary provider, a single mother responsible for his entire well-being.

When I was 34 years old, giving birth to my second son, Collin, didn't seem too daunting. Happily married with a good family, I was by then an experienced mother. I felt confident overall, yet at times while I was pregnant depression would creep into my psyche.

During the day it was easier not to allow persistent thoughts that something might go wrong with the pregnancy, as I had so much going in my favor. However, nighttime would often usher in the nagging question, "What if something is wrong?" Amniocentesis was available to determine certain birth defects, and a woman could choose to take the morally questionable test. For instance, amniocentesis can cause a spontaneous abortion if the needle is inserted in the wrong place. To some, it is also taking God's will (the potential for a deformed child) and putting the decision of what to do in human hands. If the test results indicate deformity, the mother must decide about an abortion within a few days because the birth defects test is performed four months into the pregnancy.

After many nights of struggling I chose to do the test, hoping to quell the questions that wouldn't leave my brain. My husband and I waited for the test results, and I was relieved but saddened when the doctor reported there were two baby sacs, revealing that my body had aborted a twin sometime early during my pregnancy.

"Does my baby look okay though?" I asked, anxious to know everything I could about this wonder forming inside of me.

"Yes, your baby boy looks fine," the doctor said and smiled.

Driving home, I determined that any remaining negative feelings about the pregnancy would prove temporary as my hormones settled down. Still, caring for a child with another on the way was all-encompassing, especially as I worked full time. Both professionals, my husband and I thankfully had the means to employ good at-home childcare. With my depression behind me, all seemed well in our lives once more, and I gave birth to Collin a few months later.

Unless your baby appears ill, insurance companies call routine pediatric appointments "well baby" visits. Although I worked many long hours professionally, I'd always taken Brandon to the doctor for these appointments because I loved hearing my pediatrician declare "He's fine" after the examination. Brandon had always been supremely healthy, and I was accustomed to hearing good news from my doctor. None of the babies in my family had ever experienced any noteworthy childhood illnesses, except for occasional common cold.

When I took Collin for his four-week routine check-up, I had similar expectations of being in and out of the office in no time. When the nurse finished examining him, the baby and I waited for the doctor consultation. I was growing annoyed that the appointment seemed to be taking so long and had planned to drop the baby off at my house before returning to work. Now I feared I would be late.

Thinking I had only ten to fifteen more minutes to spare before resuming my busy day, a list of to-dos consumed my thoughts. To my surprise the doctor entered the room without her ever-attendant smile. Her demeanor was serious this time, making me pay closer attention to her words.

"There seems to be something wrong with his heart," she said flatly. A fog of misunderstanding immediately surrounded me, my heart racing and stomach queasy. "Please repeat that," I asked meekly.

"It appears his heartbeat is erratic," she explained. The doctor was neither stern nor sympathetic; she was factual. I suddenly couldn't breathe and began shaking, trying to stay calm and hold Collin securely in my arms.

"What do you think it is?" I asked. I felt faint, trying not to scream at her or her nurse. The room was spinning and stifling hot. I was glad to be sitting or my weakened limbs could have dropped my son.

The doctor casually looked up from her notepad. "I don't know," she said and resumed taking notes. "I'm going to make him an appointment with a pediatric surgeon at Children's Hospital in Dallas."

Visions of bald cancer-stricken children in hospital waiting rooms raced through my brain. *No, not my child. He can't be sick. He looks fine.* Reassuring thoughts came to mind, but none would stay with me for any length of time.

"The nurse will call you when we get the appointment. It sometimes takes a while to get in," she added. Before she left the exam room, I lightly pleaded with her to please get us in as quickly as possible. Living with the unknown seemed unbearable. I left the doctor's office, placed Collin on a bench in the hall, and sat down beside him, crying quietly. I put my ear to his little chest, faintly hearing him breathe. "Please dear God, not my child," I prayed as I silently screamed inside. "He can't be sick. He looks fine!"

My overstuffed calendar suddenly seemed silly and irrelevant. I didn't care about anything but the health of my child—not issues at work, not important meetings. I tried to call my husband but couldn't reach him for several hours. When I got home I placed the baby on my bed instead of in his crib, not wanting him to be that far from me. I lay next to him, placing a wet cloth on my searing hot forehead. Maybe I would die too if anything was wrong with him.

I couldn't go on in this emotional state and craved some form of mental relief. As the baby slept, I reached into my past and could hear Mother's impassive voice: "Life goes on. Whatever it is, we'll deal with it."

Her resolve was still somewhere in my genes, and I knew that this baby and I would survive somehow. Jaw set, I clinched both fists and told myself, *I will fight for my baby. I'll take him to every heart doctor and hospital I can find. Collin has my genes too. He will prevail.*

Hearing him cry at night thereafter while we waited for the appointment I panicked, thinking his heart might have stopped. I no longer allowed him to sleep in his crib. I kept him by my side in my bed. Any movement on his part would wake either his dad or me, and we spent restless nights making sure the baby was breathing before we dozed.

The doctor finally confirmed an appointment at Children's Hospital in Dallas. Seeing my small baby's chest covered with so many tubes and monitors during their battery of tests once more brought tears. Bruce and I were asked to wait in the next room, and it seemed like an eternity until the pediatric cardiologist entered our area.

"He has an unusual hole between his lower ventricles. Usually a hole is between the upper chambers, not the lower ones. I can hear blood gushing between the two walls." The doctor seemed concerned but was soothing in his pronouncement.

"What do we do now?" I asked, not knowing if relief or panic should set in.

"Nothing yet," he stated. "Let's wait a while and monitor his progress. If the hole gets bigger or doesn't close fairly soon, we will have to perform heart surgery."

Bruce and I looked at each other in a state of confusion, worry, and slight shock. We had never contemplated our child having defects. We were silent on the way home. Doing nothing seemed a cowardly way to proceed. How could we do nothing for the child we both loved deeply? It was a question that went unanswered for months and even years as we waited and watched.

Collin was a near perfect baby in his temperament and attitude. I watched carefully to see if he gained motor skills and performed tasks at the appointed times set forth by baby experts. Crawling, babbling, walking—all seemed normal. We went for cardiology check-ups every three months, but the diagnosis remained the same. The hole had not enlarged, but it had not closed either. The cardiologist seemed more concerned with every visit. I was resigned that a surgery was near.

When Collin turned three, he began soccer and T-ball like other boys his age. I worried about his exertion, but the doctor told us to keep him active. Another check-up and another anxious afternoon brought a sudden change in the doctor's demeanor. He smiled as he approached us in the waiting room this time. "Collin has shown us all his determination," he said proudly. "The hole has grown together. He will not have to have heart surgery."

"What does this mean, Doctor?" I asked. Not yet believing what I was hearing, I implored him to give me more details.

"It means he is like any normal three-year-old."

"Do we do anything special?" I could hardly accept what he was telling me.

"No, nothing. Go home, kiss your little boy and thank God for his help and Collin's strong will." And just like that, it was all over. I hugged the doctor in relief and cried.

Walking out of Children's Hospital carrying Collin in my arms, I saw other mothers sitting with their babies wrapped tightly in blankets, waiting for some doctor to predict life or death for their future. Worry had left me as abruptly as it had come years before, but seeing these children and their parents ushered in a wave of sorrow.

"Thank you, God!" I sighed and drove home, calling my mother to tell her about our miracle. She was happy but not surprised.

"I knew with God's help that Collin could do it. Thank you, Jesus," Mother called out to her divine comrade. Then she stopped abruptly. "Donna Jene, did you thank Jesus?"

I knew I had thanked God but I wasn't sure I had included Jesus. "Yes, Mom," I said as I smiled into the phone.

Cancer

HAVING ANOTHER FEMALE MANAGER TO TALK TO was a special treat for me when I worked at Boise Cascade Corporation in 1989, managing their Dallas and Austin sales force. Men held all the other management positions, except the purchasing manager, who was a tough and capable woman. We were an unlikely pair to strike a friendship, me a smiley sales manager, her a stoic and detailed accountant. But we developed a close bond.

I loved stopping by her office early before the day started. Coffee cup in hand one day, we were laughing at a silly office situation when she looked at me squarely and said, "What's that bump on your neck?"

"Oh," I replied, trying to underplay the obviously noticeable swelling that I had seen in the mirror over the past few weeks. "I think it's probably a lymph gland. I've had a sore throat all spring. My allergies seem to be getting worse."

She scowled at me. "You should have that checked out."

"I will, if it gets worse," I said, laughing off her concern.

A few weeks later it was time for my gynecology visit. My gynecologist noticed the swelling immediately. As he felt my neck he said, "I think it's a good idea to go to an ear nose and throat man."

His nurse made my appointment. The specialist palpated the lump on my neck and concluded that a biopsy was in order. "It will leave a little scar on your neck," he cautioned.

"That's okay," I affirmed, never considering I might get many more scars in a few weeks.

A week later, his office called. The doctor wanted to go over my biopsy with me. Could I come in?

Irritated to have to leave work to go to his office, I tried not to show my agitation. I had children at home, a good corporate job, and a to-do list I would never accomplish.

The biopsy looked a little "peculiar," he said. I remember pondering his choice of words. "I think we should do an exploratory surgery," he said.

Surgery? Now I'd have to be off work for sure and likely have an even bigger scar to show for it. But vividly remembering my mother's cancer 25 years before, I relented to his advice.

His office set the date for my surgery for the following week. Later, I called my mom to inform her of what was going to happen. Ever the nurse, she insisted she would be there during the surgery. I knew my mother too well. She was coming not so much to be with me but because the doctor might need her advice. She was certain that I would.

* * *

ON THE DAY OF my surgery I kissed my three-year-old Collin and hugged my teenager Brandon. I assured them that I'd be home the next day. "Ma Ma will spend the night with you at my house," I said. All seemed fine.

Nothing is as relaxing as the medication the anesthesiologist administers. Ambivalent about the exploratory nature of the surgery, I thought I'd get a good rest if nothing else. It was not as if they had found anything definitive and were going in to remove it. They were just having a look around out of an abundance of caution, I thought.

The next thought I had after succumbing to the anesthesia was a chipper nurse bidding me good morning the day after. My husband and my mother were by my bed. I was thoroughly taped around the throat area but could still murmur, "Did everything go okay?"

I asked with confidence, but then I saw clouds in their eyes. My mother couldn't wait to be the informant. "You have cancer," she said bluntly.

What? I was stunned. Cancer? Not me, not someone my age! Although I'm a mother, I'm still a daughter. I'm too young for cancer.

My emotions went into overdrive. What if I die? Who will raise my sons?

Before I could think my surgeon appeared beside my mother.

"We got some of your malignant tumors," he said. "But we found one wrapped around your vocal cord. Before I would remove it, I wanted to explain to you that removing this tumor is tedious and dangerous. If I make a mistake and slice your vocal cord while shaving the tumor, you could possibly not speak again."

I stared at him as if he were speaking a foreign language to me. "You need to make the decision," he said as he looked at me directly. He knew I was scared. I knew he was scared. Even my mother was scared.

"Do you think the tumor in my vocal cords is malignant?"

"I don't know," he answered truthfully. "If it is malignant and we don't remove it, you will probably die from it."

I looked at my mom, remembering her bravery during a bout with cancer 25 years earlier. She nodded at me and me at her. I felt strength coming from this simple exchange, fueling the innate desire to live for my children.

"Go back in," I told him.

Within minutes I was on a gurney headed back in for another throat surgery. I didn't know if I'd ever speak again. My eyes filled with tears, but the thought of leaving my children was overwhelming. Speaking or not, I wanted to see them grow up.

Several concurrent surgeries that summer left me weak and frail. The doctors were unsure if they got everything, so I endured several treatments of radiation, one so intense that it left me in the hospital for several days. No one entered my room without a lead apron on. It's daunting to have so much radiation in your body that others can't touch you. My sore throats allowed me only a liquid diet and I lost weight rapidly.

I was more watchful and attentive of my boys during those summer months of recovery. Every trip to the doctor was stressful. Each time, I wondered what would I do if the doctor gave me only a few months to live.

Would I plan a trip around the world? Maybe I'd visit all the people

I knew to say goodbye. In the end I realized I'd do nothing different than what I was already doing before my cancer. I'd allow my boys no disruptions in the trajectory of their lives and I'd simply watch them grow and mature like any other mother would do.

Brandon was close to earning his Eagle Scout badge, an award most Boy Scouts work toward throughout high school. I was so proud of him. He went to his honor court at just thirteen years of age, but they told him he needed more leadership training and a couple of years' maturity.

He came home disappointed and we both cried. But within a few minutes, I saw evidence of the familiar pattern of my mother's will and determination in my boy. He straightened up and said, "I'm gonna get it when I'm fifteen." And he did.

I've never worried about him since. He is a reliant, self-sufficient, and determined husband and father. I know he'll be okay no matter what happens to me.

My little one, Collin, was so small. I knew he'd be okay also because my husband, Bruce, was a good father. I trusted that he'd raise him adequately, but perhaps without my sense of adventure and liberal views. But I didn't worry about his well-being with his dad.

Cancer came again like a wave on the ocean that summer. A myriad of additional exams discovered cervical cancer, stage three. Surgery again. This time it was chemotherapy. I lost twelve pounds in a few weeks.

So sick I could hardly get out of bed, I still managed to do some simple household chores to create a sense of normalcy for my family. I loved to fold my son's clothes. I could sit on my bed and touch their shirts and socks. What a pleasure to have their things in my hands and smell the fresh detergent. If I could do nothing else I hoped to be able to fold their clothes for years to come.

Mother stayed with me a short while, but we both eventually agreed that my needy father needed her more than I did. Bruce left for work each day, Brandon to middle school, and Collin to preschool.

On Saturdays the boys and their father were busy playing sports or going to other school activities. Brandon was always good at entertaining himself, Bruce coached little league soccer and T-ball, and Collin played whatever sports a three-year-old could play. Saturday was just another day of recovery for me.

Almost thirty years after my fight with two cancers, I recall deciding then that there must be a God—when I woke up from the first surgery, God was my first thought. I remember thinking that every headache must be brain cancer, every soreness had to be carcinoma, any mole had to be melanoma. The cancer mentality wins for years, but eventually fades. A normal life does return.

I wear one badge of cancer prominently. I'm sure the scar under my chin is often mistaken for plastic surgery, and how I wish that were true! But the scar reminds me of how close I came to death during my cancer recovery.

* * *

A HOT SATURDAY AFTERNOON in June left me wanting a cool shower, and I slowly crept from the bed to the bathroom. I needed to let Bruce or the kids know I was up, but decided that the walk to find them was too much for my weak body. Bruce spent Saturday afternoons working in the yard. Loud rock and roll music from his "boom box" and a cigar always accompanied him. Our big golden retriever loved to lie close by in the shade.

I undressed, sitting carefully on the side of the tub. My throat bandages needed to stay dry, so I positioned the showerhead low as to not dampen the sutures or the gauze. I stepped in the shower, hot water stinging my body until I reached for the cold spray. My next memory was that of waking up and seeing red running through the water on the shower floor. Was that my blood? What was I doing lying half in and half out of the shower?

Blood gushing from my neck, I realized that I had fainted and couldn't stand up. Without quick help, I'd soon bleed to death. I crawled through the water and blood mixture on the shower floor, blood trailing a path behind me. I was so weak that my knees were wobbling. I finally pulled myself up by the bathroom door handle. Grabbing a towel nearby, I thrust it under my chin. It was soaked within seconds.

I had to get Bruce's attention. I needed help immediately.

Opening the back door, the wide, concrete porch looked ominous. *I must not faint again*, I told myself. I could die there and my kids could find their mother's body. Music blaring and the wind blowing hard, it was difficult for me to get my husband's attention. Three or four steps onto the porch, Bruce saw me. Running toward me to see what happened, he looked aghast to see blood spurting from my chin and neck. He hurried me to the SUV and raced to the Baylor Hospital emergency room eleven miles away.

My determination to take care of myself almost cost me my future. I had lost a lot of blood and torn my sutures, creating a large gash under my chin too. The doctor said that I had hit the floor directly on my jaw and concluded that "it was God's will" that I hadn't broken my neck. After all I'd been through, if the doctor said it was God's will, who was I to question? I knew emphatically that I now believed in God, so why not thank him for his part? I also thank Bruce for looking up from his cigar. But this time I didn't thank the wind—I overcame it.

Divorce and Betrayal

J ANUARY IN NORTH TEXAS IS UNPREDICTABLE, BUT the 25th January that I spent married to Bruce proved more unpredictable than I could have ever imagined. One Friday night that month, the north wind blew hard and the evening's darkness came early. Arriving home later than my husband, I saw his SUV parked in the back driveway. He loved smoking cigars and futzing with the plants in the yard, so I assumed that's where he was. I walked through the house and out the back door to find him. I noticed that his cell phone was lying precariously on the brick ledge.

With the wind gusting, I worried that the phone might blow off the bricks and was going to move it when the phone began to vibrate, signaling that an email had come through. Without thought I picked up the phone, looking to see if it was anyone he should call back.

A shock ran through my body like an electric current. My heart pounded and I began shaking. The message was from someone whose name I did not recognize. It read, "I feel better today." I scrolled up to Bruce's earlier message that read, "How are you doing?"

To my surprise, in earlier threads they both had exchanged, "I love you's." My stomach felt queasy and my breath stopped. I quickly returned the phone to its former position on the bricks when I saw Bruce walking toward me.

Without greeting him I said, "I am going upstairs." I practically ran up the staircase to our shared bathroom. I felt faint as hot tears formed in my eyes. Betrayal. Delivered by an electronic device. This was the 21st century.

Bruce walked in the bathroom and went in his closet to change clothes because we were supposed to go out to eat.

I said, "Bruce, who is [naming the woman in the email]?" He turned toward me and stammered a bit. I could tell he was stalling for time. "I don't know. Uh, there's a woman by that name that cuts my hair. And one that is a realtor in town."

Through my tears I looked at him and asked, "Do you love this woman?" He knew that I knew.

Not answering directly, anger broiled up in his voice and he said, "You've been looking at my messages." For the life of me, to this day I still don't understand my response to him.

My mouth uttered the words, "I am sorry, I didn't mean to." My brain felt betrayed at that moment. *What? You apologized to the father of your son for uncovering his message to another woman? Twenty-five years of work, time, love, and devotion down the tubes and you're apologizing?*

Years of intellectualizing the scenario since have led me to believe that maybe my gut was telling the truth. I *was* sorry that I'd uncovered the truth. Before this happened, ignorance was bliss. I had thought our sex life was less because we were both older and working hard. I'd planned our retirement relentlessly, thinking we'd live on a golf course and Bruce would be a golf marshal, something he'd always said he wanted to do.

Everything went through my mind at once that night. I asked him to sit with me in the den. I wanted to talk, yet I also wanted sit quietly and let my shock settle in. I softly proposed, "If you'll get rid of her, we will stay together."

He agreed. I was relieved.

We both got in his SUV and just as always, went to dinner. It was quiet and strained. We came back home and I went to bed and he watched TV. I assumed he called her later and told her that I knew.

In the months that followed I blamed myself for his starting a relationship with someone else. Never content with myself, I was always the controller—the one reaching higher and wanting to achieve more. Feigning a high degree of independence, the truth was that I needed Bruce. He was level-headed and consistent but had grown more aloof through the years. Although married, we lived two separate lives. My opinion was that Bruce blamed me for the divorce.

My son Collin was at Baylor University. I knew that Bruce loved our two boys, and I thought I could appeal to his fatherhood and love of family. I wanted to keep our 26-year relationship intact. True to form, Bruce did not argue or disagree at the time.

By May I sincerely hoped we would stay together. The entire family went to Boston to see me receive a diploma from Harvard Business School. My best friend since childhood, Diane, accompanied Bruce and Collin on the plane to meet me. I was already in Boston with my older son, Brandon, and my daughter-in-law, Trisha.

Before they arrived in Boston, another best friend, Betty Jean, called me at the Four Seasons Hotel and said, "Bruce filed for divorce. It was in the paper today." Somehow I remained calm and got through the graduation ceremony the next day. I later learned that the woman was moving to our area. I believed that she had remained in his life throughout our months of discussing forgiveness. They moved in together and their relationship lasted only a few months. Ours was shattered.

I loved Bruce. He was a great father and patient husband. I had been comfortable with the idea of growing old with him. Bruce had been a fabulous athlete in high school and college and loved reliving those days. He and this woman had dated in his earlier life, and I felt certain that being with her helped him relive the fun and frivolity of his youth.

I was devastated. This time that darned north wind had set me up for a cold reality. My retrieving his phone before it blew off that brick ledge had announced that our time together had ended.

PART 4

Impossible Love

DIVORCED IN MY FIFTIES, I NEVER EXPECTED TO FALL in love again. However, if love happened, I would be open to it. I believe that love is impossible to define. What is love and how do we know when it's real? I believe I have loved a few men, each a different kind of love, but love nonetheless. One of my loves was not a husband, but a familiar stranger. A stranger, as I knew very little about this man, although something about his presence drew me to him whatever the circumstance.

Koi no yokan is the Japanese term for the sudden knowledge that upon meeting someone, you know you are destined to be together. The Japanese had me pegged perfectly. I knew that we were destined. With politics and my marriage to Bruce long finished, I was forced to start a new life's chapter, so I had returned to business with a passion. What a wonderful surprise—eventually my new job introduced me to the man who would become my new love.

In any language or culture, love gets our attention—and sometimes when we're least expecting it. The Norwegians also have a word for the overwhelming, euphoric feeling you get when you are falling in love with someone: *forelskelse*. I looked for reasons to be near this man, laughing and loving him more with each encounter. I silently cursed the Starbucks barista for taking too long making my morning coffee. Every minute counted, and I looked forward to getting to work because of the possibility of working with this man on a project.

I loved all of him: his head, his laugh, and his sloped shoulders. My heart throbbed when the workweek ended, as I knew I might not see him during the weekend. We spent Saturdays and Sundays texting and emailing our love for the other. I slept with the phone by my pillow for the first time in my life. How I cherished the ping of a new message, hoping for a new connection! Mondays were always hopeful, as a new week promised the potential of seeing him again. When work brought us together, it seemed like play. We were so good at playing. Like children, we planned for our play times. Every encounter with him brought new adventures, even if it was merely a joke or a knowing smile shared between us.

He had been single for several years, and neither of us felt remorse or sorrow that we'd loved before. I felt only exhilaration that I was his chosen one. My mind placed us together in impossible scenarios, knowing that we both had children who might limit the possibilities. Still, I dreamed of being with him anywhere and everywhere. This must have been the deepest of love, this delirious desire to be in the presence of your lover and eagerly do whatever he wants. It was, I believed, the essence of unselfishness.

Many years have passed since the days of our love. The Portuguese have a word to describe my state after our relationship ended: *saudade*. It means the intense longing for a person you love but who is now gone, leaving you with a haunting desire for that person that will never again be quenched.

The fateful Saturday that forever took us apart was originally planned as another familiar play day. His face showing a slight frown, he casually mentioned that his children were suffering over his divorce. He hated that they lived so far away from him. This, he said, was causing him great heartache. These life-altering words, merely a mumble, gave me a sudden queasiness knowing that things were about to change drastically. Instantly, I felt shattered.

He tried to let me down easy with a logical yet emotional explanation. "My children have to come before anyone else," he ventured, "so I guess I'll move closer to them." My heart hurt as though a prince had taken his sword and mortally wounded his princess. I knew our love couldn't withstand breaking the hearts of our young. They needed our protection. Staying in Dallas would lead him to resent me and eventually me him. His faint whisper of heartache signaled our end.

It was the word *onsra* from the Boro language of India that fit my feelings as I cried, kissing him in an elevator for the last time. Knowing that one's love will no longer last, loving for the last time is that bittersweet Boro word for which there is no English equivalent. On a nearby balcony as I watched him walk to his car several floors below, I stepped close to the railing. Overwhelmed and distraught, death crossed my mind. If I jumped, would the wind carry me to him again? My heart lurched forward toward him, but he was in his car in an instant, the taillights shining as the car backed out—leaving me behind forever.

L'esprit de l'escalier. The French say it best. At that moment I experienced the overwhelming feeling that there were still things we needed to talk about but knew we'd never again have the chance to. Just then the wind whipped a leafy fern off its stand and I jumped back away from death as I snapped back to reality. I had an entire life waiting ahead of me: children, aging parents, and myself to attend to. I'd miss him. *Goodbye, my love.*

I can only turn to another culture to describe how it feels whenever my mind drifts back to those days of Shakespearean tragedy. *Razbliuto.* It's Russian for the sentimental feeling that I sometimes have when I remember how much I used to love him but no longer do.

My life would reveal new possibilities, as I'm sure did his. I didn't realize it at the time, but a new love was in my future who would become my husband Herb. It was the British poet laureate, Alfred, Lord Tennyson, who once said, "'tis better to have loved and lost than never to have loved at all." I'm forever grateful that I have loved, lost, and loved again.

"Cancer of the Penis"

M Y BOYS AND I OFTEN REMARKED HOW MY PARENTS would both probably live for a hundred years. Mom and Dad, although aging and getting a bit frailer, maintained solid minds and fairly healthy bodies as they aged. When Daddy had cataract surgery and eye implants, he could once again read and enjoy his cherished books and newspapers. Mother made sure that both she and Dad stayed busy. By this time my brothers were single—Lee had been divorced for decades and Wayne was a widower—so they could spend lots of time with our parents.

Mother continued having all of us over for Sunday lunch each week. One July Sunday when we gathered at their home for this tradition, the weather delivered its typical Texas promise of stifling heat and a faint breeze. Mother remarked how hot it was in the kitchen but, never one to fail her grown children, had been cooking all morning. Mother served fried chicken, gravy and mashed potatoes, and my favorite peach cobbler. Daddy had the Sunday paper strewn over his favorite chair.

Mother summoned us to the table while the food was hot. My brothers were kidding around as usual and had made sure to hide my favorite piece of part of the bird, the wishbone. From the time I was a kid, I always wanted the wishbone. Although we were grown, they still thought of me as their little sis. This Sunday the dining room table discussion was lively as usual. My dad loved politics, probably because my grandfather supported many politicians, especially Senator John Tower. Yellow Dog Democrats, Mom and Dad changed in the 1980s for Ronald Reagan but reverted to Bill Clinton in the 1990s. As he reached for another piece of chicken, Daddy casually remarked that he and Mother were like Texas armadillos—they were politically going down the middle of the road these days. This was his way of saying that they once again had gone Republican, voting for George W. Bush.

If this Sunday meal was any different, it escaped me. I was busy worrying that I was getting older and that Mother's peach cobbler was adding pounds around my midsection. Mother typically left the table before dessert and started clearing leftovers. This day she pulled a chair up beside Daddy at his end of the table. I assumed Daddy was going to tell some new story. It turned out that it was her with news.

During a lull in the conversation, Mother abruptly announced, "Your daddy has cancer." For a brief second the room was silent. Daddy didn't say a word, but looked at the table like he was ashamed. The three of us, now reduced to our parents' children, sat there in different states of shock. I asked first, "What kind of cancer?"

Mother looked serious but couldn't contain her sense of humor. "Cancer of the penis," she said, almost animated. We weren't sure whether to believe her, as she loved pranks, but cancer was too serious for even her antics.

"The penis?" Lee was stunned. "I've never heard of that." He looked pale. Wayne was perplexed, still half-believing what he was hearing.

"Did he overuse it making us kids?" I couldn't help making a joke.

"Probably," she responded. Slight chuckles floated around the table before Mother further informed us of the details of what was wrong with our father. "But the cancer is real. Daddy is having surgery in two weeks at the Catholic hospital in Wichita. We figured he would be safe there, as those nuns won't cause his penis any problems."

Mother's stalwart sense of humor was easing the tension. How strange that we were all laughing at Dad's misfortune.

"How serious is this?" I asked, having regained my worry.

"We don't know, but they'll probably cut off part of it." Mother was doing all the talking. We all snickered again.

I couldn't help myself and blurted out, "Mother, what's that going to do to your sex life?" My brothers didn't seem surprised with our banter. Mother had raised us to be realists aware of Mother Nature, and farm life had taught us well about the birds and the bees.

Smiling, she looked at Daddy and said, "I guess it's about time your daddy gets circumcised." We didn't know whether this 85-year-old woman was kidding or not this time. Daddy looked at her and returned the smile. I felt weird. Mother could do that to us—make us feel weirded out sometimes.

"Do I need to come for the surgery?" I asked tentatively. At this time I was still serving as mayor, and my calendar was loaded the following week. Thankfully, both Lee and Wayne were retired so they agreed they'd both be at Bethania Hospital for Daddy's later-in-life circumcision.

* * *

THE NEXT FRIDAY THE surgeon cut off a few inches of Daddy's penis. Between city meetings I called Mother late in the day to see how everything went. She had promised to call me if anything happened during surgery. Things can happen to a ninety-year-old like Daddy during an operation.

"All went well," she reported. "However, they are not sure they got it all."

"What does that mean?" I held my breath, imagining the worst. Mother explained that they might have to do more surgery. "But not yet," she added. I promised her I would be at the hospital the next day to check on my dad.

"Mom, are you all right?" I asked before hanging up.

She acted surprised by my question. "Of course I am. I've never had a penis to get cut off," she deadpanned. "See you tomorrow." She hung up.

Walking across the Bethania Hospital parking lot the following day, I felt the pavement's searing heat and worried that my sandals might get black tar on them as the asphalt appeared to be melting on that hideous July afternoon. Daddy appeared in good spirits, but was groggy. Ever the caregiver, Mother assumed her role as the health authority, letting me know that she had everything under control. Since the doctors rarely visited his room, she instructed the nurses on how to care for Daddy. She had nurse's training and was an expert on my dad. After a few hours I left to drive back to Colleyville, feeling as I always had since childhood. Daddy was in good hands. Mother had control.

Daddy recuperated at home. I never asked how one recuperates from this kind of surgery, but Mother teased him relentlessly about his reduced stature. Daddy was good-natured, always finding my mother funny. As the months progressed, it became obvious that Daddy was not improving. He had severe pain in his right side and remained on a catheter.

* * *

WHEN THANKSGIVING ROLLED AROUND my brothers and I made plans to be out at our parents' home. It was a big holiday for our family. When I got to their house, Daddy was not in his big chair. He loved the special edition newspaper on Thanksgiving and always tuned in to the parades on television. "Where's Daddy?" I asked, immediately sensing that something was wrong.

"He's in bed," Mother said definitively. She looked at me solemnly and said, "Donna Jene, they couldn't get all the cancer. They've given him three months."

I couldn't believe it. My mother had recovered from cancer. I had recovered from cancer. Why couldn't my dad?

"Go on in there," she said, motioning toward their bedroom. "He'll love seeing you."

I felt lost. "What do I say to him?"

"Say what's on your mind," she offered. "But don't start feeling sorry for him or any of us. When it's his time, it's his time. Your daddy is saved. He'll just see Jesus before we do, unless you have a car accident on that crazy road to Dallas."

Mother never allowed anyone to feel secure. Her view was that death was always a minute away. In her mind we had to be right with God, just as Daddy was.

The picture of my dad sitting up in bed on that cold and windy Thanksgiving morning has never left my mind. Wayne was already in the room at the foot of the bed, and we all chatted for a few minutes. Daddy always wanted to know about my mayoral duties. Crazy about my two boys, he also asked about Brandon's law practice and if Collin was doing well at Baylor University. I could hear Mother in the kitchen, busy preparing Thanksgiving lunch.

I felt compelled to ask my dad some questions about his long life. Daddy was dying. It might be my last chance. "Daddy, if you could do just one more thing, or go one more place, what would it be?" I questioned him. Mother had come in the bedroom to check his bedside table and was walking back out of the room. Daddy grinned, as only he could when he knew he was going to tease Mother.

"Well, I'd have one more dance with your mother," he said weakly. At that moment, Mother turned toward him and retorted flippantly, "What makes you think I'd want to dance with an old man like you?" With that, she left the room. "She always has to have the last word," he smiled faintly.

I cried. Wayne cried. Daddy sat silently. "Everyone will be okay," he assured me. "Now go help your mother and let's have some good food."

I remember thinking, "My God. Most children never get to hear the ending of a 69-year-old love story." How their father, quiet and stoic, enjoyed years of pleasure with his strong-willed, energetic woman. How he had lived much of his life through her humor and passion. This last declaration of love was the best gift a dad could give to his daughter. For that I can never thank him enough.

Daddy died January 4, 2004.

He and Mother meticulously planned the funeral, paying for everything in advance. I'm sure that Mother covered most of the details the way she wanted as Daddy lay in bed, happily compliant. I didn't need to worry about my mother's emotional well-being. She got through the funeral with few tears. She knew that Daddy was going to heaven. Always one to enjoy a party, she relished seeing old friends at the visitation.

When we went back to what we would now call "Mother's house," she went to her closet to take off her funeral clothes. I had asked her why she chose to wear a blue knit suit instead of black. She told me that blue was Daddy's favorite color. I felt tears stinging my eyes once more. We visited just a minute more and then as I prepared to leave, I was concerned that she'd be lonely.

"Mother, will you be all right now that Dad's not here? What will you do tomorrow?"

"I'll go to Wal-Mart." She was emphatic. Thinking she might need something, I asked if I needed to take her today before I left.

"No, I don't need anything. But I plan to go to Wal-Mart every day. Those old men at the front of the store—the greeters? They might be perfect boyfriends. You know, friendly and working ... what more can a woman ask for? I need to check them all out."

"Mother!" I gasped, thinking of my father's freshly dug grave at the cemetery.

She laughed a bit wickedly and shooed me out the front door to get on my way back home. We never had reason to believe that Mother ever dated another man, although she loved to tease us about her secret sex life with the Wal-Mart greeters. We sort of didn't believe her, but with her you never were one hundred percent sure.

Fire's Damnation

"**L**IFE'S NOT OVER YET. WE'LL JUST SEE WHAT HAPPENS next."

That's what my mother said to me when I called her on New Year's Eve and joked that she would be the youngest ninety-year-old in Texas in 2006. We didn't know it then, but that New Year's Day would change all our lives profoundly.

Power lines from decades ago stretched across the grassland where I grew up. It brought electricity to outposts across Texas, including the dotted farms and ranches near the Red River. Like all people raised in the country, we were aware of the dangers of high-voltage electricity from downed wires, which caused grass fires and occasionally killed a lineman attempting to restring the lines.

Winter winds were always expected in the area, and the New Year brought powerful gusts. A severe drought had parched the land, requiring ranchers to bring in water and food for their livestock throughout the season. It also necessitated that Sunday churchgoers regularly add rain to their prayer lists. But God seemed to ignore West Texas and the drought worsened. The potential for a grassfire was near perfect at the start of 2006.

On a lonely stretch near Henrietta, Texas, the power lines had weakened through years of what was probably oversight at best and neglect at worst. The fragile lines whipped in the wind, one finally wrangling loose and sending sparks across the parched pasture. Not a soul was nearby this isolated area, and the fire had its heyday before anyone became aware.

My brothers were with Mother on the holiday. Wayne would later recall how noisy the wind was as they watched the TV lineup of football games and parades. He walked outside to his car and saw faint smoke coming from the west. The sight was not unusual in the wide stretches of Texas. We all learned to mostly ignore it, as it seldom affected the ranches and homes.

A closer look revealed that this smoke was different; it seemed to be rolling in the wind, looking angry like a spring tornado. Still not too concerned, he mentioned the smoke to Mother and promised to monitor it from the west kitchen window. It had been fifty-odd years since a fire had completely destroyed my childhood home, and Mother was still terrified of fire.

"Wayne, can you smell it?" she wanted to know, taking deep breaths through her nostrils. She looked at my brother, scared of what might be lurking in the black northern sky. "I can," she insisted, "so it must be close for me to be able to smell it."

To assuage her fears, Wayne went outside again to inspect the situation, Mother and Lee following behind him. Using binoculars, they could see red flames shooting in the air. To their horror they realized that several fiery areas had merged and a wall of fire was now approaching rapidly. Grass fires rarely damaged houses as they slow down once they hit the green grass afforded by the sprinkler systems that surrounded most homes. Green grass and water are godsends to ranchers when fighting hellacious firestorms. Still, the drought-bitten prairie was perfectly hospitable to the incessant wind winging the fire-breathing dragon closer to civilization. Thinking quickly and taking no chances, Wayne decided to spray down the roof and foundation of the house.

As my brothers doused Mother's home, the flames continued to rage, looking angrier with each mile they devoured. This fire was deadly and Wayne acted swiftly to take Mother and Lee and drive away from the flames. My brothers dashed inside the house to grab essentials and found Mother with her family Bible in tow and her purse, packed and ready to flee the path of destruction. They hurriedly discussed what else to save in case the fire won this battle. As usual Mother led the conversation when Wayne heard an ominous crackle.

"Mother, we have to get out *now*!" he demanded.

Mother hesitated before adding, "Wait a minute. I need my hearing aid." As she walked by the kitchen window, flames engulfed the tree just beyond the glass. The warning was clear: "You're next if you don't run now." And run they did!

The flames quickly lapped up two sides of the house as they made their way outside. Both cars were parked in the south side garage, black smoke billowing near the kitchen door.

"Where are the keys?" Wayne shouted. Finding a set of keys on the hall table, he threw open the kitchen door. The fire, dangerously near the cars, thanked him for an easy entrance to the home and barged its way in.

Lee, having wrapped his jeans in wet towels, bounded for the backseat of one of the cars. In an instant Mother was in the passenger's seat. Wayne worried about starting the gas engine. The fire was wide and fast, offering no obvious way to outrun it. Nevertheless Wayne gunned the car backward into the blackness. Miraculously, the car didn't burst into flames, but instead cooperated to get them to safety.

They headed south about a mile away, all the while breathing the choking smoke. Out of harm's way, they got out of the car and tried to clear their tired lungs. For 89 years Mother had been adept at evading this devil, and it seemed as if she had escaped its clutches once more.

"God saved us," she told her sons between coughs. "Now which one of you wants to take Jesus in your heart?" My mother's determination to save her children never took a break. Baptism by fire was a very real concern for my family in the country, but only Mother took it in a spiritual, not necessarily literal, sense.

* * *

NO ONE IN MY family cried that day. Alive, they could face losing their belongings, but the alternative was not an option. The small town near where my mom lived was devastated as the rolling monster inflamed by Texas winds roared through the tiny burg. Fireballs careened through the old houses, charring the dried wood and eating the innards of people's homes.

My brother Lee had been just seconds from death. The fire was so hot and so close that the plastic earpieces on his glasses had melted on his face, burning the tops of his ears. Once more, decades of family pictures were destroyed in Satan's furnace, along with souvenirs of family trips, awards for sports, and everything else acquired through my mother's long life together with my dad.

Several rural firefighters were burned battling the blaze, but fortunately none died. Forty fire departments fought the fiery beast for three days. Thousands of acres of pastureland and farms lay scorched and worthless in its wake.

The next day after the fire, I drove to what remained of my mother's house. My family had been walking through the leftover ashes since daylight. I stopped the car and ran to hug my mother and brothers. My brothers' tears were rare, but this time they freely rolled down their dirty cheeks. Wayne said they'd stayed in a small motel in Bowie, Texas, the night before but could only get one room for everybody.

I was terrified that this total loss late in life would kill my mother's soul and then her body. But I saw no tears on Mom's face. As I talked with my brothers, she continued to rummage a bit in the rubble without picking up one piece of charred salvation.

I insisted that everyone go for breakfast and coffee, realizing that all of our nerves needed quieting. After our meal I felt compelled to probe for any emotional trauma I was sure my mom must have been feeling. "Mom," I began with tears welling in my eyes, "I'm so relieved you made it out. What a blessing." I felt that God had once again tested these hardy souls and pushed them to the human limits. Two fires five decades apart, coupled with my daddy's death.

I wondered what more an 89-year-old woman could endure. Mother made no response to my overture.

"Well, I guess God was really testing our family once again," I blurted out. Silence continued for a few seconds.

"This was not a test, but God's blessing," she finally stated resolutely. "God gave us a reminder how important we are as a family."

I absently looked out the dirty window of the tiny café and noticed raindrops settling on the hood of my car. Having spent my youth with incessant wind blowing over the cracked earth sections of West Texas land, I knew that the rain would make everything better.

"But Mom, what will you do?" I asked, insisting for my own sake to know that her resolve was intact. My mind raced through the possibilities of where she would live and how she would ever recover from this blow.

"What do you mean?" She smiled briefly. "I only have one choice now. I'll have to go to Wichita tomorrow. I hope one of the boys will take me. I've got new furniture to buy."

That was vintage Mother—the positive realist who knew each day brought new hope. With no place to live, she was miles past that part of her problem. She was already considering her next endeavor. Never one to fold her tent, she was already planning her new décor. It would be two more years before she died, succumbing to a stroke at the age of 92. I remember so vividly what she had always told me: "Life goes on. That's God's way."

The wind has a prevailing presence in this book for a reason. Sometimes center stage and at other times a bystander with bit parts, it has consistently been part of my existence for more than six decades, blowing as innocently in wreaking terror as it did when caressing my face. I often wonder how my life would have been different without its continued presence, but I guess I will never know.

EPILOGUE

How fortunate I was to be born into my family's kaleidoscope. I'm grateful to each of them because I know they contributed to, and often deserve credit for, who I am.

My mother, Coy Lee, was a forthright, controlling, and generous woman. Her difficult upbringing and early life experiences may have hardened her "reality evaluation" antennae. I simply know that she kept our family permanently stuck on trial. Every day Mother assessed our accomplishments, then loved us and criticized us. Our reality was typically scored with humor. Her passion, grit, and determination were constants in the unsteady environment she created.

Daddy was an engaged bystander who adored his family and took delight in our lively household, although he frequently retreated to his books and television. Daddy exhibited strength when he defied his parents to marry my mother and raise my sister as his own.

My sister, Billie, would often make poor choices but was a kind woman. She never meant to harm anyone and had a great sense of humor. Her love of her family remained until she died of emphysema at 75.

My brother Lee was bright and funny. He had the most trouble loosening Mother's apron strings. His death certificate lists the cause of death as undiagnosed, but I believe he died of loneliness and a broken spirit. Years of being divorced, coupled with the death of Mother, Dad, and our brother, Wayne, sucked the life from him at 72.

Wayne was my idol and my biggest cheerleader. Sometimes God needs a special angel, so He took Wayne by colon cancer at 63. I will never recover from his death.

My grandfather Tom was an enormous influence on all who knew him. Wise, strong, and balanced, he was the rock I needed. Grandmother Lennie was quick on compliments and had a way of making me feel better than I was. My grandparents' love and respect for each other was obvious. No individual could break their bond, match their devotion, or question their unity. Grandmother never changed, even though she was totally blind at age 83 and died of age-related issues at 95.

My sister-in-law Linda was a sister to me. She and Wayne were truly one, and I adored both of them. Linda's infectious laughter still rings in my ears.

My oldest son, Brandon, taught me what a mother's love can be. As a single mother, I wished for Brandon to grow up to be an independent, confident, and self-sufficient man. At 41, he is an accomplished attorney, Texas Aggie, Eagle Scout, mayor, and admirable father and husband. I am immensely proud of him and often regret my inability to adequately convey to Brandon the happiness and love he has brought to me.

My youngest son, Collin, overcame early health problems and has grown into a fine man. He exudes loyalty and acceptance to all. Creative, humble, and non-threatening, Collin continuously moves his goals forward. After graduating from Baylor University he earned an MBA and is a successful entrepreneur. Collin has the unique ability to make others feel important. I have undying love for him and take great joy in having watched him mature so beautifully.

* * *

WRITING MY MEMOIR WAS more difficult than I expected. In revisiting my past, I rediscovered my life's bumps and bruises earned during my six decades and have learned that my experiences were easier than some and more difficult than others.

My mother was a huge influence in my life, and although she contributed to my insecurities, she also afforded me an adventurous soul. My grandfather's entrepreneurial success and positive influence gave me reason to feel secure in my small pond in Texas. My family expected my academic achievements, but they never considered that I would enter the business world. I had no training for the roles I assumed in the decades after college. Becoming a young woman in the Seventies granted me a minor part in the Women's Movement. I endorsed my role of often being "the first"—the first woman to do whatever. I told anyone who asked if I was a feminist that I was an opportunist. If the opportunity presented itself, I was eager to give it a try. I mostly ignored the fabled glass ceiling, yet kept chipping away at it.

Yet even with business success, entrepreneurial conquests, and my graduation from Harvard Business School OPM, I still searched for something to fulfill me. My sons, Brandon and Collin, have always been an enormous sense of pride, but I regretted that their mom was always struggling in her own head, thinking surely there was more that I could achieve.

Only since I reached my sixties have I felt at ease with life. Years of anxiety that accompanied my soul have lessened. With the help of my dear friend Betty Jean Willbanks, I finally accepted that I am stronger and more resilient than I had ever believed. Betty Jean would often say, "Donna, listen to me. You are free and can do anything you want. Enjoy life!" My fear of failure finally gave way to the sense that I've done okay! Her unconditional love helped me to define the nemesis lurking throughout my childhood and adulthood: an overriding desire for approval and need to achieve in order to please.

My readers, before I began writing I committed to an honest assessment of my past, knowing that I would likely face criticism and possibly upset others. But I wrote about my life as I remember it, often inserting my own opinions.

While I searched for fulfillment, purpose, and peace in life, I was blessed to always be able to keep going. I've found that growth comes in strange and unexpected ways.

The details of my future remain unknown, but I feel certain of two facts. Although the Texas wind brushed me with fires, blowing snow, hot gusts, and cool breezes, I have decided that it is good to have a constant companion reminding us that change is inevitable so we should embrace it. Second, I know that my future will always be a work in progress.

I hope to meet you again on a written page and will definitely be back looking for you. I promise to share the rest of my story, if you'll be so kind as to read it.

One by One, You Left

You timed it so well, my daddy dear;
You said good-bye as we all stood near.
You shared us your thoughts as ne'er before
As Mom walked by and closed your door.

"If I could have one just one more dance
I'd twirl your mom, never looking askance.
Our youth we'd once again relive,
My love again to her I'd be willing to give."

My dearest Wayne, you left far too early;
Your smile, your laugh, I loved you dearly.
It's hard to say that I have no brothers
Especially you, who provided my innocence such comfort and cover.

I know if there are those heaven bound;
You're up there with God and looking down.
My birthday heart aches every December,
When you'd hide my gifts and pretend not to remember.

My mother, how I loved you, but you left me your way;
To death you controlled it, refusing to stay.
Your joy, your laughter, your feelings so deep,
These gifts that you gave me, I'm so happy to keep.

So many strengths and so much love to give;
God tested your soul and you loved to live.
But as you held my hand when Daddy just died,
You assured me you're with me while I sat down and cried.

My brother, Lee, how tough you were,
Hanging on too long, with death hovering so near.
Your body had left you but your mind wouldn't go;
No pain, but peace, I longed for you so.

Every time in this world I choose to compete,
I think of my Lee, urging me to unseat
Whatever competitor might get in my way;
You were my best cheerleader—"keep going" you'd say.

My sister, Billie, you were a force
Making your own way, never afraid of divorce.
I never doubted you loved your family,
Your children, your parents, and us three siblings.

I miss you all, my loving family ghosts;
Not one of you do I miss the most.
I know you're with me sometime every day;
I love you and thank you is all I can say.

Without you I just wouldn't be me;
Maybe better and smarter and stronger I'd be.
Our blood ran together, our lives intertwined;
I look forward to good times, but love looking behind.

A family is precious,
Our time was so fast.
Never thinking much about it,
But our time didn't last!